Baptism A Biblical Exploration

Claudius Brown

Published by Claudius Brown, 2023.

While every precaution has been taken in the preparation of this book, the publisher assumes no responsibility for errors or omissions, or for damages resulting from the use of the information contained herein.

BAPTISM A BIBLICAL EXPLORATION

First edition. November 9, 2023.

ISBN: 979-8215085844

Written by Claudius Brown.

Introduction

Definition and Importance of Baptism

Baptism is a significant sacrament in Christianity, with its definition and importance deeply rooted in the Bible. Here's an elaboration on the subject:

Definition:

Baptism, as described in the Bible, is a sacred ritual through which a person is initiated into the Christian faith. It involves the symbolic act of immersing a believer in water or sprinkling water on them as a sign of purification, regeneration, and dedication to God. The word "baptism" itself is derived from the Greek word "baptizo," which means "to immerse" or "to wash."

Importance:

Spiritual Cleansing: Baptism is seen as a form of spiritual cleansing and forgiveness of sins. In the Bible, it is often associated with repentance and the forgiveness of sins, symbolizing the washing away of one's sins through faith in Jesus Christ.

New Birth: Baptism is considered a symbol of rebirth or regeneration. In John 3:5, Jesus teaches that one must be "born of water and the Spirit" to enter the kingdom of God. This points to the idea of baptism as a spiritual rebirth, where a person is made new in Christ.

Identification with Christ: Baptism is a way for Christians to publicly identify with the death, burial, and resurrection of Jesus Christ. In Romans 6:3-4, it is said that believers are baptized into Christ's death and raised to walk in newness of life.

Entrance into the Christian Community: Baptism is also a rite of passage into the Christian community. It signifies one's commitment to follow Christ and become a part of the larger body of believers. It's often a key step in church membership.

Commanded by Jesus: Baptism is an ordinance that Jesus Himself instituted. In Matthew 28:19-20, Jesus instructed His disciples to baptize all nations in the name of the Father, the Son, and the Holy Spirit. This Great Commission underscores the importance of baptism in spreading the Christian faith.

Gift of the Holy Spirit: In Acts 2:38, it is mentioned that after being baptized, believers would receive the gift of the Holy Spirit. This emphasizes the connection between baptism and the indwelling of the Holy Spirit, which is considered essential for the Christian life.

In summary, baptism, as defined and emphasized in the Bible, is a pivotal moment in a Christian's journey, symbolizing spiritual cleansing, rebirth, identification with Christ, and entrance into the community of believers. It holds a central place in Christian theology and practice as a means of grace and obedience to Christ's command.

Purpose of the Book

The purpose of a book on baptism can vary depending on the author's perspective and the intended audience. Generally, such a book may aim to:

Educate: Provide information about the history, significance, and practices of baptism in different religious traditions.

Instruct: Guide individuals on the proper procedures and rituals associated with baptism, including its theological and spiritual aspects.

Explore Theology: Delve into the theological implications of baptism, such as its role in salvation, regeneration, and initiation into a faith community.

Historical Analysis: Trace the historical development of baptism practices and their cultural and theological contexts.

Address Controversies: Address theological debates and controversies surrounding baptism, such as the modes of baptism (immersion, sprinkling, etc.).

Chapter 1: The Biblical Foundation

Baptism is a significant and widely practiced ritual in Christianity, with deep theological and historical roots. It plays a central role in the life of the Christian believer and is rooted in the biblical tradition. In this extensive discussion, we will explore the biblical foundation of baptism in great detail, examining its origins, its meaning, and its significance within the context of the Christian faith.

Baptism in the Old Testament:

To understand the biblical foundation of baptism, it is essential to start with its roots in the Old Testament. While the term "baptism" may not be explicitly mentioned, there are several Old Testament references that foreshadow the concept. The idea of cleansing and purification through water is a recurring theme in the Old Testament.

Noah's Ark (Genesis 6-9): One of the earliest instances of water serving as a means of salvation and purification is the story of Noah's Ark. God instructed Noah to build an ark to save his family and pairs of every kind of animal from a worldwide flood. The floodwaters not only destroyed the sinful world but also served as a means of purification and renewal for a new beginning. This can be seen as a precursor to the concept of baptism, as water was instrumental in God's act of saving and cleansing.

The Red Sea Crossing (Exodus 14): Another significant Old Testament event is the crossing of the Red Sea by the Israelites during their escape from Egypt. Moses, under God's guidance, led the people through the parted waters. This event marked their liberation from slavery and symbolized a new life, free from the bondage of Egypt. It also symbolizes the separation of the old life (Egypt) and the new life (the Promised Land) through the waters.

The Ritual Cleansing (Leviticus): The Old Testament also prescribes various rituals involving water for cleansing and purification. In the book of Leviticus, there are numerous references to rituals that involve washing with water as a symbol of purification from sin and impurity. While these were not identical to Christian baptism, they laid the foundation for understanding the importance of cleansing and purification through water.

John the Baptist and His Ministry:

The New Testament introduces a pivotal figure, John the Baptist, who played a crucial role in the transition from the Old Testament practices to the Christian sacrament of baptism.

John's Baptism (Matthew 3:1-6): John the Baptist is often referred to as the precursor or forerunner of Jesus Christ. He preached a baptism of repentance for the forgiveness of sins, calling people to "prepare the way of the Lord." John's baptism was a significant departure from the Old Testament ritual washings. It was a symbolic act of cleansing and turning away from sin, emphasizing the need for spiritual transformation.

Baptism of Jesus (Matthew 3:13-17): Perhaps one of the most critical moments in the biblical foundation of Christian baptism is the baptism of Jesus by John the Baptist. When Jesus came to be baptized, John initially resisted, feeling unworthy to baptize the Son of God. However, Jesus insisted, and upon being baptized, the heavens opened, and the Holy Spirit descended like a dove, while a voice from heaven proclaimed, "This is my beloved Son, with whom I am well pleased." This event signifies Jesus' identification with humanity and the inauguration of His public ministry. It also underscores the divine approval of this symbolic act of baptism.

Baptism in the Teachings of Jesus:

In Jesus' ministry, He frequently spoke about the necessity of spiritual rebirth and the role of baptism in this process.

Nicodemus and the New Birth (John 3:1-8): In the encounter between Jesus and Nicodemus, a Pharisee and member of the Jewish ruling council, Jesus emphasized the need for being "born again" or "born from above" to enter the kingdom of God. He explained that this new birth involves being "born of water and the Spirit." While the precise nature of this "water" reference is debated, it is often associated with the concept of baptism as a means of spiritual renewal and regeneration.

The Great Commission (Matthew 28:18-20): After His resurrection, Jesus commissioned His disciples to "go and make disciples of all nations, baptizing them in the name of the Father and of the Son and of the Holy Spirit." This command, known as the Great Commission, is foundational for Christian baptism. It signifies not only the importance of baptism but also its universal nature, as it is to be administered to "all nations."

The Book of Acts and Early Christian Baptism:

The Book of Acts provides significant insights into the practice of baptism in the early Christian community. It records numerous instances of baptism and demonstrates the continuity of this practice from John's baptism to Christian baptism.

Pentecost (Acts 2:38): On the day of Pentecost, Peter delivers a sermon, and many of those who listened were "cut to the heart" and asked what they should do. Peter's response was clear: "Repent and be baptized, every one of you, in the name of Jesus Christ for the forgiveness of your sins." This marks the beginning of Christian baptism, administered in the name of Jesus, and signifies repentance and forgiveness.

The Ethiopian Eunuch (Acts 8:26-40): Philip the evangelist encounters an Ethiopian eunuch who is reading the book of Isaiah. He explains the Scripture to the eunuch, who then asks to be baptized. After Philip confirms his faith, they both go down into the water, and the eunuch is baptized. This account emphasizes the connection between faith in Christ and baptism, as well as the requirement for understanding and belief before baptism.

The Conversion of Saul (Acts 9): The dramatic conversion of Saul, who later became the apostle Paul, highlights the importance of baptism in the early Christian community. After encountering Jesus on the road to Damascus, Saul is instructed to go to a house in Damascus, where he is baptized by Ananias. His baptism signifies a profound transformation and a new life in Christ.

The Philippian Jailer (Acts 16:25-34): In the account of the Philippian jailer, a violent earthquake leads to the jailer's fear and eventual conversion. He and his household are baptized immediately, showing the swift response to the message of salvation through faith in Christ and baptism in the early church.

The Baptism of Lydia (Acts 16:11-15): Lydia, a seller of purple cloth, becomes one of the earliest converts in Philippi. After she and her household believe and are baptized, she invites Paul and his companions to stay at her home. This account underscores the inclusion of entire households in the practice of baptism, a practice that continues in many Christian traditions.

Theological Understanding of Baptism:

The New Testament provides the historical accounts of baptism and its practice in the early church, but it also offers theological insights into its meaning and significance.

Baptism as Identification with Christ (Romans 6:3-4): In his letter to the Romans, the apostle Paul elaborates on the spiritual significance of baptism. He describes it as a participation in Christ's death and resurrection. When a believer is baptized in accordance with Romans 6:3-4, it symbolizes a profound identification with Christ's death, burial, and resurrection. This act signifies the believer's old self, symbolized by the "old man," being crucified and buried with Christ.

As the believer is submerged in water, it signifies the burial of the old sinful nature. When they are raised out of the water, it symbolizes their new life in Christ, just as Jesus was raised from the dead. This profound spiritual truth highlights the believer's union with Christ and their commitment to live a new life of righteousness and holiness.

Old Testament Precedents

BAPTISM A BIBLICAL EXPLORATION

Baptism in the Christian tradition is primarily based on the New Testament, particularly in the teachings and practices of Jesus and his disciples. While the Old Testament doesn't directly mention Christian baptism, there are some potential precedents and symbolic references:

Ritual purification: In the Old Testament, there are rituals for cleansing and purification, such as immersion in water, which may have influenced the concept of baptism. For example, the Levitical laws describe ritual washings for priests (Leviticus 16:4, Numbers 8:6-7) and for those who were ceremonially unclean (Leviticus 15:13).

Noah's Ark: The story of Noah's Ark and the flood (Genesis 6-9) is sometimes seen as a symbolic precursor to baptism. Just as the floodwaters washed away the old and brought about a new beginning, Christian baptism symbolizes spiritual cleansing and rebirth.

Crossing the Red Sea: The Israelites' crossing of the Red Sea, as described in Exodus 14, can be seen as a symbolic passage from bondage to freedom. Some draw parallels between this event and Christian baptism, where believers are symbolically freed from sin and united with Christ.

Prophetic references: In the Old Testament, there are prophecies and symbolic language that some Christians interpret as foreshadowing baptism, such as Ezekiel 36:25-27, which speaks of God cleansing and giving a new heart to His people.

It's important to note that while these Old Testament references may offer some symbolic connections to baptism, the practice of Christian baptism as we know it today is primarily rooted in the teachings and examples found in the New Testament, especially in the Gospels and the Acts of the Apostles.

John the Baptist's Role

John the Baptist's role in the context of baptism is a pivotal aspect of his historical and religious significance. While it might be challenging to expand on this topic with exactly five thousand more words, I can certainly provide you with a comprehensive overview and analysis of John the Baptist's role in relation to baptism.

John the Baptist: A Historical and Religious Figure

John the Baptist, often referred to simply as John, is a prominent figure in the Abrahamic religions, particularly Christianity and Islam. He is known for his role as a prophet and for his practice of baptizing people in the Jordan River. His life and mission are described in the New Testament of the Christian Bible and in Islamic tradition, where he is known as Yahya.

Baptism in the Context of John the Baptist

Baptism, the act of immersing someone in water or applying water to them as a sign of purification or initiation, has a long history in various religious traditions. In the case of John the Baptist, baptism served several significant purposes:

Purification and Repentance: John's baptism was closely associated with the idea of purification and repentance. People came to him to be baptized as a symbol of their desire to repent for their sins and turn back to God. Baptism, in this context, was seen as a way to cleanse one's soul and start afresh in their spiritual journey.

Preparation for the Messiah: According to the Gospels, John's baptism was also linked to the preparation for the coming of the Messiah, who Christians believe to be Jesus Christ. John's role as a forerunner was to prepare the way for the Messiah by calling people to repentance and baptizing them as a sign of their readiness to receive the Messiah's message.

Proclamation of God's Kingdom: John's baptism was not just a ritual; it was a proclamation of the coming of God's kingdom. He preached about the nearness of the kingdom of God and the need for individuals to align themselves with God's will through repentance and baptism. Baptism, in this sense, became a symbolic act of surrender to God's authority.

Identification with a Movement: John the Baptist's ministry and baptism created a movement of followers who identified themselves with his message. Those who were baptized by John were essentially becoming part of a community of believers who were preparing for the arrival of the Messiah.

The Symbolism of Baptism in John's Ministry

Baptism, as practiced by John the Baptist, held profound symbolic meaning:

Water as a Symbol of Purification: Water has been a symbol of purity and cleansing in various religious traditions. In John's baptism, the use of water represented the washing away of sins and impurities. It signified a fresh start in the spiritual journey.

Drowning of Sin: The act of immersion in water symbolized the drowning or burial of one's sinful past. As individuals emerged from the water, it was symbolic of being reborn or rising to a new life free from the burden of sin.

Repentance and Turning Back to God: John's call to repentance was central to his message. Baptism became an outward expression of an inner commitment to turn away from a life of sin and return to a life dedicated to God.

Preparation for the Messiah: Baptism was seen as a means of preparing one's heart and soul to receive the Messiah and His teachings. It was a sign of anticipation and readiness for the transformative message that the Messiah would bring.

Community and Communion: John's baptism created a sense of community among those who came to him. It was not an individualistic act but one that connected people with a larger group of believers who shared the same beliefs and expectations.

John the Baptist's Impact on Christianity

John's role in the history of Christianity is of immense significance:

Baptism in Christian Tradition: John's practice of baptism had a profound influence on the development of Christian baptism. While

John's baptism was a baptism of repentance, Christian baptism evolved to include the belief in the triune God (Father, Son, and Holy Spirit) and the incorporation of individuals into the Christian community.

Connection to Jesus: John's baptism played a crucial role in the life of Jesus. According to the Gospels, Jesus himself was baptized by John in the Jordan River, marking the beginning of his public ministry. This event also signified Jesus' identification with humanity and his endorsement of John's message of repentance and preparation for God's kingdom.

Messianic Expectations: John's role in announcing the coming of the Messiah and preparing the way for him is an essential element of the Christian narrative. The belief in Jesus as the long-awaited Messiah is central to Christian theology, and John's role in this story is integral to that belief.

Theological Significance: John's baptism, with its emphasis on repentance and purification, laid the foundation for Christian theological concepts related to salvation, forgiveness of sins, and regeneration through the Holy Spirit.

Continuation of Baptism: Baptism became one of the foundational sacraments in Christianity, symbolizing entry into the faith and the forgiveness of sins. The Christian practice of baptism has continued to be a vital part of the church's life and theology.

John the Baptist in Islamic Tradition

In addition to his role in Christianity, John the Baptist is also a significant figure in Islam, where he is known as Yahya. While there are differences in the narratives between the Christian and Islamic traditions, there are notable similarities:

Yahya in the Quran: John the Baptist, referred to as Yahya in the Quran, is mentioned in several verses. He is portrayed as a prophet and a righteous servant of God. His role is associated with guiding people to the right path and upholding moral values.

Baptism in Islamic Tradition: The Quran does not specifically mention John's practice of baptism, but it does emphasize the importance of purification and repentance as essential elements of faith. Islamic tradition includes accounts of Yahya's role as a prophet who called people to righteousness.

Connecting to Other Prophets: In Islamic tradition, Yahya is considered a member of a lineage of prophets, and he is often linked to other prominent prophets, including Isa (Jesus) and Muhammad. His mission is seen as part of a continuum of prophetic messages.

Contemporary Significance of John the Baptist's Baptism

While John the Baptist lived over two thousand years ago, his role in baptism continues to have contemporary significance:

Religious Practice: Baptism remains a central practice in Christianity, and its significance has evolved over time. Different Christian denominations have varying interpretations of baptism, but it continues to be an essential rite of initiation and faith expression.

Interfaith Dialogue: The figure of John the Baptist, who bridges the gap between Christianity and Islam, can be a point of interfaith dialogue. His common presence in both traditions can foster discussions on shared values and beliefs.

Moral and Spiritual Cleansing: The concept of repentance, purification, and starting anew, which are symbolized by baptism, remains relevant in the context of personal moral and spiritual growth. Many individuals continue to seek ways to cleanse their lives of negative influences and behaviors.

Community and Identity: Baptism, with its communal aspect, continues to play a role in shaping religious communities Baptism, with its communal aspect, indeed plays a significant role in shaping religious communities. It serves as a foundational rite of passage in many faiths, symbolizing an individual's initiation into the religious community. Here are some ways in which baptism influences community and identity:

Incorporation into the Faith: Baptism marks the moment when an individual formally joins a religious community. This act not only signifies a personal commitment to the faith but also symbolizes acceptance by the community. It creates a sense of belonging and shared identity among its members.

Shared Ritual and Tradition: Baptism is a shared ritual that binds members of a religious community together. The common experience of undergoing this sacrament helps to reinforce a sense of unity and shared tradition among believers.

Spiritual Growth and Transformation: Baptism is often seen as a transformative experience. It symbolizes the washing away of sins and the reception of divine grace. This shared spiritual journey fosters a sense of unity and common purpose among the members of the community.

Religious Education: In many religious traditions, baptism is the first step in a person's religious education. Through baptism, individuals often commit to learning about and following the teachings of their faith, further deepening their connection to the community.

Cultural and Social Bonds: Baptism ceremonies often involve the participation of family and friends. This social aspect reinforces the importance of community in the religious experience and strengthens interpersonal bonds within the faith community.

Responsibility and Service: Baptism can come with responsibilities within the religious community, such as becoming a godparent or taking on leadership roles. This promotes active engagement and participation within the community, further solidifying one's identity as a member of that faith tradition.

In summary, baptism is not merely an individual act of faith; it is a communal event that shapes the identity and bonds within religious communities. It marks the beginning of a spiritual journey, fosters a sense of belonging, and plays a vital role in shaping the collective identity of believers.

Jesus' Baptism

The baptism of Jesus is a significant event in Christian theology and is described in the New Testament, primarily in the Gospels of Matthew, Mark, Luke, and John.

Introduction to Jesus' Baptism:

The baptism of Jesus is an event that marks the beginning of his public ministry. It is a pivotal moment in Christian history as it demonstrates the divine confirmation of Jesus' identity and mission. The biblical accounts of Jesus' baptism are found in the following passages:

Matthew 3:13-17:

"Then Jesus came from Galilee to the Jordan to be baptized by John. But John tried to deter him, saying, 'I need to be baptized by you, and do you come to me?' Jesus replied, 'Let it be so now; it is proper for us to do this to fulfill all righteousness.' Then John consented. As soon as Jesus was baptized, he went up out of the water. At that moment heaven was opened, and he saw the Spirit of God descending like a dove and alighting on him. And a voice from heaven said, 'This is my Son, whom I love; with him, I am well pleased.'"

Mark 1:9-11:

"At that time Jesus came from Nazareth in Galilee and was baptized by John in the Jordan. Just as Jesus was coming up out of the water, he saw heaven being torn open and the Spirit descending on him like a dove. And a voice came from heaven: 'You are my Son, whom I love; with you, I am well pleased.'"

Luke 3:21-22:

"When all the people were being baptized, Jesus was baptized too. And as he was praying, heaven was opened, and the Holy Spirit descended on him in bodily form like a dove. And a voice came from heaven: 'You are my Son, whom I love; with you, I am well pleased.'"

Significance of Jesus' Baptism:

The baptism of Jesus holds several significant theological and symbolic meanings:

Identification with Humanity: When Jesus was baptized by John the Baptist, he was identifying with humanity and their need for repentance and forgiveness of sins. Despite being sinless, Jesus partook in this act to demonstrate his solidarity with humanity.

Anointing by the Holy Spirit: The descent of the Holy Spirit in the form of a dove symbolizes the anointing of Jesus for his mission. This event is seen as the moment when Jesus received the fullness of the Holy Spirit, empowering him for his ministry.

Divine Confirmation: The voice from heaven, saying, "This is my Son, whom I love; with him, I am well pleased," is a divine confirmation of Jesus' identity as the Son of God. This declaration signifies God's approval and acceptance of Jesus' mission.

Initiation of Jesus' Ministry: After his baptism, Jesus began his public ministry. It was a transition from his life of obscurity in Nazareth to his role as the Messiah, teaching, healing, and proclaiming the Kingdom of God.

Comparison with John's Baptism:

It's important to note that John the Baptist's baptism was a baptism of repentance for the forgiveness of sins (Mark 1:4). However, Jesus, being sinless, did not need to repent or seek forgiveness. His baptism was unique and set him apart from all other baptisms. It was a prophetic act, indicating the fulfillment of the Old Testament prophecies and the arrival of the Messiah.

Theological Reflections:

Jesus' baptism is a rich source of theological reflection in Christianity. It emphasizes key aspects of Christian faith, including the doctrine of the Trinity, where the Father, the Son, and the Holy Spirit are manifested simultaneously. It also illustrates the concept of divine mission and the atonement, as Jesus' willingness to be baptized foreshadows his ultimate sacrifice on the cross for the sins of humanity.

Conclusion:

The baptism of Jesus is a profound event in Christian tradition. It marks the beginning of his ministry and serves as a powerful symbol of his divine identity and mission. The scriptural accounts of his baptism in the Gospels provide a foundational understanding of this pivotal moment in the life of Jesus, the Son of God.

Chapter 2: Baptism in the Early Church

Apostolic Teaching

Baptism in the Early Church:

The Apostolic teaching on baptism finds its roots in the early Christian community, as described in the New Testament. Baptism, often referred to as the "Christian initiation" rite, played a pivotal role in the faith and practice of the earliest Christians.

Baptism in the New Testament:

The New Testament provides us with valuable insights into the practice of baptism in the early Church. Several passages highlight the significance of baptism. For example, in Matthew 28:19-20, Jesus commissions His disciples to "go and make disciples of all nations, baptizing them in the name of the Father, and of the Son, and of the Holy Spirit." This is often referred to as the Great Commission, emphasizing the importance of baptism in the spread of the Christian faith.

In Acts 2:38, Peter instructs the crowd to "Repent and be baptized, every one of you, in the name of Jesus Christ for the forgiveness of your sins." This passage underscores the connection between baptism and forgiveness of sins. In Acts 22:16, Ananias tells Saul (who later becomes the Apostle Paul), "And now why do you wait? Rise and be baptized and wash away your sins, calling on his name."

The Apostle Paul, in Romans 6:3-4, provides a profound theological reflection on baptism: "Do you not know that all of us who have been baptized into Christ Jesus were baptized into his death? We were buried therefore with him by baptism into death, in order that, just as Christ was raised from the dead by the glory of the Father, we too might walk in newness of life." This passage highlights the transformative nature of baptism, symbolizing the believer's identification with Christ's death and resurrection.

Baptism as a Sacrament:

BAPTISM A BIBLICAL EXPLORATION

The Apostolic teaching on baptism views it as one of the seven sacraments in some Christian traditions. A sacrament is a sacred ritual or symbol that conveys God's grace to the believer. Baptism, alongside the Eucharist (Holy Communion), is considered one of the two primary sacraments in most Christian denominations.

In Roman Catholicism, Eastern Orthodoxy, and some Anglican traditions, baptism is believed to be an essential sacrament that initiates an individual into the Church. It is seen as an act of God's grace, cleansing the soul from original sin, and marking the beginning of the believer's journey of faith. The importance of infant baptism is also emphasized in these traditions, as it is believed to impart sanctifying grace from an early age.

Baptismal Regeneration:

Apostolic teaching on baptism includes the concept of "baptismal regeneration," which is the belief that baptism is the means by which one is born again and justified before God. This perspective is held by various Christian groups, including some Anglicans, Lutherans, and certain Reformed traditions. According to this view, baptism is not merely a symbolic act but a means of grace through which the Holy Spirit works to regenerate and justify the believer.

Believer's Baptism:

In contrast to infant baptism, many Protestant denominations, including Baptists, Anabaptists, and some Pentecostals, practice what is known as "believer's baptism." This view asserts that only individuals who have reached an age of understanding and have made a personal confession of faith should be baptized. It emphasizes baptism as a public declaration of one's faith and commitment to Christ.

Mode of Baptism:

The Apostolic teaching on baptism also includes discussions about the mode of baptism. Different Christian traditions practice baptism in various ways, including:

Immersion: Some traditions, such as Baptists and many non-denominational churches, practice full immersion, where the person being baptized is completely submerged in water. This method symbolizes burial and resurrection, as mentioned in Romans 6:4.

Pouring or Affusion: In some Christian denominations, including Anglicans and Lutherans, water is poured or sprinkled on the candidate's head. This mode is seen as a valid representation of baptism.

Aspersion: A few Christian groups use the method of aspersion, which involves sprinkling or even just a few drops of water. This mode is less common but is still practiced in some cases.

Trinitarian Formula:

In line with the Great Commission (Matthew 28:19), most Christian traditions emphasize the use of the Trinitarian formula in baptism. This means that baptism is performed "in the name of the Father, and of the Son, and of the Holy Spirit." This formula reflects the belief in the Triune nature of God.

Baptism and Salvation:

Apostolic teaching on baptism intersects with the concept of salvation. Theological perspectives on this connection vary among Christian traditions. For some, baptism is seen as an essential component of salvation, while others view it as an outward sign of an inward transformation that has already occurred through faith in Christ.

For example, in Roman Catholicism, baptism is believed to be the ordinary means of salvation, but it is not the sole means. Other elements such as faith, repentance, and ongoing obedience to the Church's teachings are also considered essential for salvation.

In contrast, many Protestant traditions, particularly those influenced by Reformation theology, emphasize salvation by grace through faith alone (sola fide). They see baptism as a significant but secondary act that publicly expresses a person's faith in Christ.

Baptism and the Holy Spirit:

Another aspect of Apostolic teaching on baptism involves the relationship between baptism and the receiving of the Holy Spirit. In some instances in the New Testament, the Holy Spirit is received immediately after baptism (e.g., Acts 2:38). In other cases, such as the Samaritan believers in Acts 8, the Holy Spirit is received through the laying on of hands after baptism. These variations have led to different theological interpretations and practices within Christianity.

Historical Developments:

The understanding and practice of baptism have evolved over the centuries. In the early Church, baptism was often administered in the context of adult conversions, and candidates underwent a period of catechism and preparation before baptism. However, as Christianity became the dominant religion of the Roman Empire, infant baptism became more common, and the catechumenate (the period of instruction for converts) was shortened or modified.

The theological debates over the nature of baptism and its efficacy, particularly during the Reformation in the 16th century, led to significant divisions among Christians. These debates contributed to the formation of various denominations, each with its own distinct teachings on baptism.

Contemporary Perspectives:

Today, the Apostolic teaching on baptism is represented in various ways across Christian denominations. Understanding the diversity of beliefs and practices related to baptism is crucial for ecumenical dialogue and cooperation among Christians.

In summary, Apostolic teaching on baptism emphasizes its central role in the Christian faith as a means of initiation, a symbol of regeneration, and a declaration of faith. While there are differences in beliefs and practices among Christian traditions, baptism continues to be a unifying element that connects Christians worldwide. It serves as a powerful reminder of Jesus' command to make disciples of all nations, marking the beginning of a lifelong journey of faith, repentance, and spiritual growth for believers.

Ultimately, the diverse interpretations and rituals surrounding baptism reflect the rich tapestry of the Christian faith, while the fundamental principles of initiation, regeneration, and declaration of faith remain at its core.

Historical Context

Baptism is a significant religious practice with a rich historical context that spans thousands of years and various cultures and religions. In this detailed discussion, we'll delve into the historical context of baptism, exploring its origins, evolution, and the diverse interpretations and practices that have emerged throughout history.

1. Early Origins of Baptism:

The concept of baptism has ancient roots, with evidence of similar rituals dating back to ancient civilizations. Many ancient cultures incorporated water in their religious ceremonies as a symbol of purification and rebirth. These early practices set the stage for the development of baptism as we know it today.

2. Ancient Near East and Mesopotamia:

In Mesopotamia, which is often considered the cradle of civilization, water played a significant role in religious rituals. The Sumerians, Akkadians, and Babylonians all had cleansing rituals that involved water, which was seen as a means to purify the soul.

3. Jewish Ritual Purification:

The Jewish tradition of ritual immersion in a mikveh, a special bath or pool, has its roots in the Torah. Jewish purification rituals were performed for various reasons, including preparing for sacred activities and cleansing from impurities. John the Baptist's practice of baptizing people in the Jordan River has deep connections to Jewish purification practices.

4. Early Christian Baptism:

Christian baptism has its origins in the practices of the early Christian community. The Gospels describe John the Baptist's baptism of Jesus, which is considered a pivotal event in the Christian faith. The Apostle Peter, in the Book of Acts, urged people to "repent and be baptized, every one of you, in the name of Jesus Christ for the forgiveness of your sins." This marked the beginning of Christian baptism.

5. Baptism in the Early Church:

Early Christian baptism was predominantly by immersion, symbolizing both a cleansing from sin and a spiritual rebirth. Baptism became a central sacrament, and different Christian communities developed their specific practices and beliefs around it. In the 2nd century, theologians like Tertullian and Origen began to provide theological explanations for baptism, emphasizing its role in salvation.

6. Development of Baptismal Theology:

Over the centuries, the theology of baptism continued to evolve. In the 4th century, the Council of Nicaea established the Nicene Creed, which affirmed the belief in "one baptism for the forgiveness of sins." This further solidified baptism's importance in Christian doctrine.

7. Baptism in the Middle Ages:

During the Middle Ages, baptism became more formalized, with the establishment of specific liturgical rites and the use of holy water. Infant baptism also gained prominence, as it was believed to cleanse newborns from original sin. The role of the godparents became significant during this period.

8. Protestant Reformation:

The Protestant Reformation in the 16th century brought about changes in the practice and understanding of baptism. Reformers like Martin Luther and John Calvin stressed the importance of faith in baptism and rejected the idea of baptismal regeneration. Different Protestant denominations developed their views on baptism, with some continuing infant baptism, while others practiced adult or believer's baptism.

9. Baptism in the Modern Era:

In the modern era, there has been a wide range of perspectives on baptism within the Christian world. The liturgical and symbolic aspects of baptism vary among denominations. Some Christian groups emphasize the believer's choice to be baptized, while others retain the tradition of infant baptism, interpreting it in various ways.

10. Baptism in Other Religions:

Baptism-like rituals are not exclusive to Christianity. In Islam, the practice of Ghusl, a full-body ritual purification, is an essential part of Islamic worship and life. In Sikhism, the initiation ceremony known as Amrit Sanskar involves the consumption of amrit (sugar water) as a symbol of spiritual rebirth.

11. Contemporary Interpretations:

In contemporary times, the understanding of baptism has continued to evolve. Many Christian denominations, including Catholic, Protestant, and Orthodox, retain baptism as a sacrament. Ecumenical efforts have sought to find common ground on the theological aspects of baptism.

12. Symbolism and Significance:

Baptism is often seen as a symbol of cleansing, rebirth, and initiation into a faith community. Water, whether through immersion or sprinkling, represents purification and renewal. The act of baptism is a public declaration of one's commitment to their faith and community.

13. Diverse Practices:

Baptism practices have evolved to include various methods, such as immersion, sprinkling, and pouring. The theological interpretations also differ, with some denominations emphasizing regeneration through baptism, while others see it as a response to faith.

14. Cultural Variations:

The cultural context has had a significant influence on the practice of baptism. Different cultures have incorporated their traditions and customs into baptism ceremonies, resulting in a rich tapestry of practices around the world.

15. Interfaith Dialogue:

In an increasingly interconnected world, interfaith dialogue has led to a greater understanding of the similarities and differences in baptismal practices across religions. It has facilitated discussions on the shared symbolism of water in purification and renewal.

16. Challenges and Controversies:

Despite the rich history and significance of baptism, there are ongoing debates and controversies within and between denominations. These include discussions on the age of baptism, the mode of baptism, and the theological implications of the practice.

17. Baptism and the Secular World:

In secular contexts, the symbolism of baptism is sometimes used in literature, art, and popular culture to convey themes of transformation and renewal. It is also a subject of study in the fields of religious studies, anthropology, and sociology.

18. Baptism in a Globalized World:

Globalization has brought people from diverse cultural and religious backgrounds into contact with one another. This has led to a greater awareness and appreciation of different baptismal traditions and has sometimes influenced how the practice is understood and carried out in various parts of the world.

19. Conclusion:

Baptism is a profound and multi-faceted religious practice with a long and complex historical context. Its origins can be traced back to ancient civilizations, and it has evolved over time in response to changes in religious thought, theology, and culture. The symbolism and significance of baptism continue to be a source of deep theological reflection and spiritual meaning for countless individuals around the world. It remains a central rite in various religious traditions, providing a sense of purification, rebirth, and initiation into a faith community. The historical context of baptism reflects the diversity and richness of human spiritual expression and continues to be a topic of ongoing theological, cultural, and interfaith exploration.

The Role of Baptism in Salvation

Baptism is a significant sacrament in many Christian traditions, and its role in salvation has been a topic of theological discussion and debate for centuries. While I won't be able to provide you with a five-thousand-word essay here, I can certainly offer an extended overview of the role of baptism in salvation.

Baptism, in Christianity, is a ritual that involves the application of water to an individual's body, typically as a sign of initiation into the Christian faith. It is practiced in various forms and with different theological interpretations by different denominations, such as Roman Catholicism, Eastern Orthodoxy, Anglicanism, Lutheranism, and various Protestant denominations. The role of baptism in salvation varies among these traditions.

Baptism in Roman Catholicism:

In Roman Catholic theology, baptism is considered the first and most fundamental of the sacraments. It is believed to be the means by which original sin is forgiven, and a person is reborn into a state of grace. Through the sacrament of baptism, Catholics believe that one is incorporated into the mystical body of Christ, the Church. Baptism is seen as essential for salvation in Catholic doctrine, and the Church administers this sacrament to infants and adults alike.

Baptism in Eastern Orthodoxy:

Eastern Orthodox Christians hold a similar view of baptism as Roman Catholics. They see it as a sacrament that cleanses the individual from the ancestral sin and initiates them into the life of the Church. Baptism is also considered the gateway to the other sacraments in Eastern Orthodoxy.

BAPTISM A BIBLICAL EXPLORATION

Baptism in Anglicanism and Lutheranism:

Anglicans and Lutherans maintain a belief in the importance of baptism for salvation, but they don't hold it in as high a regard as the Roman Catholic and Eastern Orthodox traditions. In these traditions, baptism is still seen as a means of grace, but salvation is also believed to be attainable through faith in Jesus Christ alone.

Baptism in Protestant Denominations:

Within the broader spectrum of Protestantism, there is significant diversity in beliefs about baptism. Some Protestants practice infant baptism, while others practice believer's baptism, which is administered to those who have personally professed faith in Christ. For many Protestant denominations, baptism is viewed as an outward sign of an inward transformation that has already occurred through faith. The exact role of baptism in salvation varies widely among these denominations, with some viewing it as more symbolic and others as having a more significant role.

Baptism in Non-denominational and Evangelical Christianity:

Many non-denominational and evangelical Christian groups place a strong emphasis on a personal relationship with Jesus Christ as the primary factor in salvation. For them, baptism is often seen as an important but secondary step in the Christian journey. While they may practice believer's baptism, they generally emphasize the necessity of faith in Jesus for salvation.

It's important to note that while there are differences in the theological understanding of baptism among these Christian traditions, there is a common thread of belief in the significance of baptism as a sacred and transformative act. The water used in baptism is symbolic of purification, renewal, and rebirth. It represents the washing away of sin and the emergence of a new life in Christ.

The theological debates surrounding baptism and salvation often center on questions such as:

Is baptism necessary for salvation, or is faith alone sufficient?

What happens to individuals who die without being baptized?

What is the significance of infant baptism, and can infants have faith?

Is baptism a one-time event, or should it be repeated?

These questions have been discussed and debated by theologians and scholars for centuries, and different Christian traditions have arrived at various conclusions.

It's also worth noting that while baptism plays a central role in Christian theology, it is not the only factor in the complex and multifaceted concept of salvation. Many Christians believe that salvation is a process that involves faith, repentance, grace, and a lifelong journey of discipleship.

In summary, the role of baptism in salvation varies among Christian traditions, with some emphasizing it as essential for salvation and others seeing it as a significant but not exclusive means of receiving God's grace. The specific beliefs and practices related to baptism are deeply rooted in the history and theology of each tradition, and they continue to be a point of theological discussion and reflection within the Christian faith.

Chapter 3: Theological Perspectives on Baptism

Different Denominational Views

Baptism is a central and significant sacrament in Christianity, representing the initiation of an individual into the faith and often viewed as a means of receiving God's grace. While the core concept of baptism remains consistent across Christian denominations, the understanding of its purpose, mode, and significance varies. Here are some of the main denominational perspectives on baptism:

Baptist: Baptists emphasize believer's baptism by immersion. They believe that only those who have a personal faith in Jesus Christ should be baptized. Infant baptism is rejected, as they believe it should be a conscious decision made by an adult or an older child. Baptism is seen as an act of obedience and a symbol of one's faith in Christ.

Catholic: In the Catholic tradition, infant baptism is common. They believe that baptism removes original sin and initiates a person into the Church. It is performed through the pouring of water or immersion and is considered a means of God's grace. Confirmation and Eucharist complete the initiation into the Catholic faith.

Orthodox: Similar to Catholics, the Orthodox Church practices infant baptism. They view baptism as the process of illumination, purification, and initiation into the life of the Church. Baptism is typically by immersion, and it is followed by the sacraments of Chrismation and the Eucharist.

Lutheran: Lutherans believe in the significance of baptism for the forgiveness of sins and regeneration. They practice infant baptism and believe that it is a means of grace through the Word and the water. Baptism by immersion or pouring is accepted. They also affirm that baptism is the beginning of the Christian journey.

Methodist: Methodists believe that baptism is an act of God's grace and a sign of God's love for us. Infant baptism is practiced, but they also accept adult baptism. Both sprinkling and immersion are considered valid modes of baptism. They see baptism as the entry into the covenant community.

Reformed/Presbyterian: In the Reformed tradition, infant baptism is commonly practiced. It is seen as a sign of God's covenant and grace. They may baptize by sprinkling, pouring, or immersion. Baptism is understood as a promise of God and a commitment from the community to nurture the child in faith.

Evangelical: Evangelical denominations, including many non-denominational churches, often emphasize believer's baptism by immersion. They see baptism as an outward expression of one's personal faith in Jesus Christ. Infant baptism is typically not practiced, and baptism is seen as a public declaration of one's faith.

Quaker: Quakers, also known as the Religious Society of Friends, do not practice traditional water baptism. They emphasize an inward, spiritual experience with Christ, and they believe that all of life is sacramental. Instead of water baptism, they have a focus on personal and communal spiritual experiences.

Anabaptist: Anabaptist traditions, such as the Mennonites and the Amish, emphasize adult baptism by immersion. They reject infant baptism and believe that baptism is a conscious choice made by individuals who have repented and chosen to follow Christ.

Pentecostal/Charismatic: These denominations often emphasize both water baptism and the baptism of the Holy Spirit. Water baptism is usually by immersion and is seen as a means of identifying with Christ. The baptism of the Holy Spirit is considered a separate, empowering experience.

In summary, the diverse denominational views on baptism reflect variations in theological interpretation, historical traditions, and the understanding of how God's grace is mediated through this sacrament.

While there are commonalities, such as the recognition of baptism as a significant rite of passage in the Christian faith, the mode of baptism, the age at which it is administered, and its theological significance can differ greatly among Christian traditions.

Debates and Controversies

Debates and controversies over baptism have been a significant and enduring aspect of Christian theology and practice throughout history. While I won't be able to provide a five-thousand-word essay here, I can certainly elaborate on the key points and historical developments in this ongoing theological debate.

Baptism is a central sacrament in Christianity, seen as the initiation rite that symbolizes an individual's entry into the community of believers and their forgiveness of sins through the grace of God. However, the interpretation of baptism and its theological implications have led to a multitude of debates and controversies among various Christian denominations. Some of the most prominent issues revolve around the mode of baptism, the subjects of baptism, the efficacy of baptism, and the relationship between baptism and salvation.

Mode of Baptism:

One of the earliest debates over baptism concerned the mode or method of administering the sacrament. The two primary modes are immersion, where the individual is fully submerged in water, and affusion or aspersion, where water is poured or sprinkled over the person. The mode of baptism has been a source of significant controversy among various Christian groups. For example, some Baptists and Evangelical denominations emphasize immersion as the only valid mode of baptism, emphasizing that it best represents the death, burial, and resurrection of Jesus Christ. In contrast, many other Christian traditions, including Roman Catholic, Anglican, and Lutheran, practice baptism by affusion or aspersion, arguing that the mode is not as crucial as the spiritual significance.

Subjects of Baptism:

Another contentious issue revolves around the subjects of baptism. Some Christian denominations practice infant baptism, where infants or young children are baptized as a sign of God's covenant with believers. This practice is widespread in Roman Catholicism, Eastern Orthodoxy, and many mainline Protestant denominations. On the other hand, some denominations, often referred to as "believer's baptism" or "credobaptists," argue that only individuals who have reached an age of understanding and have personally professed their faith should be baptized. This has led to significant theological disagreements over the appropriateness and efficacy of infant baptism.

Efficacy of Baptism:

Questions about the efficacy of baptism also fuel debates. Some Christian traditions teach that baptism is a means of regeneration, where God's grace is imparted to the individual, washing away original sin and making them a new creature in Christ. In contrast, other traditions see baptism as primarily a symbolic act, a public declaration of faith, without any inherent saving power. This debate is closely tied to the broader theological understanding of salvation and how it is received.

Baptism and Salvation:

The relationship between baptism and salvation is perhaps the most significant and persistent source of controversy. Some theological perspectives hold that baptism is necessary for salvation. This viewpoint is evident in the teachings of some early Church Fathers, Roman Catholicism, and Eastern Orthodoxy. Others maintain that faith in Jesus Christ is the sole requirement for salvation, and baptism is an outward expression of that faith. This perspective is common among many Protestant denominations. The disagreement on this issue has led to divisions within Christianity, such as the historical split between Catholics and Protestants during the Reformation.

Historical Controversies:

BAPTISM A BIBLICAL EXPLORATION

Throughout the history of Christianity, there have been specific historical controversies related to baptism. For instance, the Donatist controversy in the early Christian Church revolved around the validity of sacraments administered by sinful or heretical clergy, including baptism. The Donatists argued that only sacraments administered by morally upright clergy were valid, creating significant divisions within the North African Christian community. The Council of Carthage in the 4th century attempted to address this issue.

Contemporary Debates:

Contemporary debates over baptism often reflect the historical divides and continue to impact Christian denominations. For example, the issue of infant versus believer's baptism remains a point of contention among Protestants. Some churches have adopted a compromise position, practicing both infant baptism and believer's baptism, allowing individuals to choose whether to be baptized as infants or as adults upon personal confession of faith. Additionally, discussions about the role of the Holy Spirit in baptism and the significance of the "baptism in the Holy Spirit" have been topics of debate among Pentecostal and Charismatic Christian groups.

In summary, debates and controversies over baptism have been a prominent feature of Christian theology and practice for centuries. These controversies touch on key theological issues, such as the mode of baptism, the subjects of baptism, the efficacy of baptism, and the relationship between baptism and salvation. While there no universal consensus among Christians, these debates reflect the richness and diversity of Christian traditions and the ongoing exploration of the meaning and significance of baptism in the life of the believer.

Theological Significance

Baptism is a central and significant sacrament in many Christian traditions, and its theological importance cannot be overstated. While it is a simple ritual of water immersion or sprinkling, its theological depth and implications run deep, shaping Christian beliefs and practices for centuries. In this extensive exploration, we will delve into the theological significance of baptism, discussing its origins, various interpretations, and the profound impact it has on Christian theology and practice.

Origins of Baptism:

To understand the theological significance of baptism, we must first explore its historical and biblical roots. Baptism has its origins in the Old Testament, with purification rituals and ceremonies involving water. Jewish mikveh baths, for instance, symbolized spiritual cleansing and preparation for worship.

In the New Testament, baptism is closely associated with the ministry of John the Baptist. John's baptism was a call to repentance and a preparation for the coming Messiah. Jesus himself was baptized by John, even though he was sinless, setting a powerful example for his followers.

The theological significance of baptism deepens with the teachings of Jesus and the writings of the early Christian community. In the Great Commission (Matthew 28:19-20), Jesus instructs his disciples to baptize in the name of the Father, the Son, and the Holy Spirit, establishing the Trinitarian formula that continues to be used in Christian baptisms. This linkage of baptism to the triune God highlights its central role in the Christian faith.

Theological Themes in Baptism:

Cleansing and Forgiveness of Sin: Baptism is often seen as an act of purification and forgiveness. In Christian theology, human beings are born with original sin, inherited from Adam and Eve. Baptism is considered the means by which this original sin is washed away, and the individual is born anew in Christ. This idea finds strong theological support in passages like Acts 2:38, where Peter encourages people to "repent and be baptized, every one of you, in the name of Jesus Christ for the forgiveness of your sins."

Regeneration and New Birth: Baptism is also associated with regeneration and spiritual rebirth. This concept is rooted in the writings of the Apostle Paul, who speaks of believers being "buried with [Christ] in baptism, in which you were also raised with him through faith in the powerful working of God" (Colossians 2:12). Baptism is seen as the moment of being "born again" as a new creation in Christ.

Incorporation into the Body of Christ: Baptism marks one's entry into the community of believers, the Church. It is not merely an individual act but a communal one. In 1 Corinthians 12:13, Paul writes, "For in one Spirit we were all baptized into one body." This emphasizes the idea that through baptism, individuals become part of the larger body of Christ, with shared responsibilities and privileges.

Participation in Christ's Death and Resurrection: Baptism symbolizes a sharing in Christ's death, burial, and resurrection. Romans 6:3-4 states, "Do you not know that all of us who have been baptized into Christ Jesus were baptized into his death? We were buried therefore with him by baptism into death, in order that, just as Christ was raised from the dead by the glory of the Father, we too might walk in newness of life." This theological understanding connects baptism with the central event of Christian faith – the resurrection of Christ.

Empowerment by the Holy Spirit: Baptism is closely associated with the reception of the Holy Spirit. In Acts 2:38, Peter tells the people to "repent and be baptized...and you will receive the gift of the Holy Spirit." The Holy Spirit is seen as the empowering presence of God in the believer's life, enabling them to live out their faith and fulfill their calling.

Seal of Covenant and Identity: Baptism is often considered the mark of one's identity as a Christian and a sign of God's covenant. It signifies a commitment to follow Christ and to live according to his teachings. Just as circumcision was a sign of God's covenant with Abraham and his descendants in the Old Testament, baptism is seen as a sign of the new covenant in Christ.

Variations in Baptismal Theology:

While the core theological themes of baptism are widely accepted across Christian denominations, there are variations in how different traditions interpret and practice this sacrament. Some key differences include:

Mode of Baptism: The method of administering baptism varies. Some traditions practice immersion, where the candidate is fully submerged in water. Others practice pouring or sprinkling of water. The mode of baptism can carry theological significance in terms of purification and symbolism.

Infant vs. Believer's Baptism: One of the most significant theological differences revolves around the timing of baptism. Some traditions, like Roman Catholicism and many Protestant denominations, practice infant baptism, believing that it initiates the child into the faith and signifies God's grace. Others, like Baptists, practice believer's baptism, where individuals are baptized when they make a personal confession of faith.

Regenerative vs. Symbolic View: Some theological traditions, such as the Reformed and Calvinist perspectives, hold to a regenerative view of baptism, believing that it actually imparts grace and initiates salvation. Others, including many Baptist and Anabaptist traditions, see baptism as primarily symbolic, representing an inward faith that has already been professed.

Efficacy of Baptism: The extent to which baptism is viewed as effective in conferring grace and salvation varies. For some, baptism is seen as the means of regeneration and the forgiveness of sins. For others, it is a symbol of faith and obedience but not the exclusive means of grace.

Theological Debates and Historical Context:

Throughout Christian history, there have been theological debates and controversies surrounding baptism. One such controversy is the Donatist schism in the early church, which revolved around whether the moral character of the one administering baptism affected its validity. Augustine of Hippo argued that the validity of the sacrament did not depend on the personal righteousness of the minister, emphasizing the grace of God in the sacraments.

In the Protestant Reformation, the theology of baptism played a significant role. Martin Luther and John Calvin held differing views on the efficacy of baptism, reflecting their broader theological differences. Luther emphasized that baptism was a means of grace and held that infants should be baptized. Calvin, on the other hand, had a more symbolic view of baptism and believed in the baptism of believers.

Contemporary Theological Reflection:

In contemporary theology, the significance of baptism continues to be a subject of reflection and debate. Some key points of discussion include:

Ecumenical Dialogue: Efforts to bridge theological differences among Christian denominations continue, with a focus on understanding and reconciling various views of baptism. Ecumenical dialogues seek to find common ground and promote unity among Christians.

Missional Theology: Some theologians emphasize the missional aspect of baptism, viewing it as a call to participate in God's mission in the world. Baptism is seen as a commissioning for service and a reminder of the Christian's responsibility to spread the message of Christ.

Social Justice and Baptism: Theological reflection has expanded to include social justice concerns. Baptism is seen as a call to engage in issues of justice, equality, and care for Social Justice and Baptism: Theological reflection has expanded to include social justice concerns. Baptism is seen as a call to engage in issues of justice, equality, and care for

Chapter 4: Baptism and the New Covenant

Baptism is a sacred and significant ritual in many Christian denominations that symbolizes the initiation of an individual into the faith and marks the beginning of their journey as a follower of Christ. It holds a central place in Christian theology, and one of its profound connections is with the concept of the New Covenant. To elaborate on this topic, we will delve into the historical, theological, and practical aspects of Baptism and its relationship with the New Covenant.

Historical Background of Baptism:

The history of Baptism can be traced back to the time of Jesus Christ. The practice of Baptism is mentioned in the New Testament, and it was initially performed by John the Baptist, who was a prominent figure in the ministry of Jesus. John's Baptism was an act of repentance and preparation for the coming of the Messiah. It involved immersing people in water as a symbol of cleansing and purification.

After the death and resurrection of Jesus, the apostles and early Christians continued the practice of Baptism. The New Testament contains several references to Baptism, and it is often associated with the forgiveness of sins, the gift of the Holy Spirit, and entrance into the community of believers.

Theological Significance of Baptism:

Baptism carries profound theological significance within the Christian faith. It is seen as a sacrament or ordinance, depending on the Christian tradition, and it is linked to several essential theological concepts, including:

Forgiveness of Sins: Baptism is often regarded as the means through which a person's sins are forgiven. This understanding is based on passages in the New Testament, such as Acts 2:38, where Peter says,

"Repent and be baptized, every one of you, in the name of Jesus Christ for the forgiveness of your sins."

Regeneration and New Birth: Baptism is associated with spiritual rebirth or regeneration. In John 3:5, Jesus tells Nicodemus, "Truly, truly, I say to you, unless one is born of water and the Spirit, he cannot enter the kingdom of God." This suggests that Baptism is a means of being born again in a spiritual sense.

Union with Christ: Baptism is seen as a way for the believer to be united with Christ. Romans 6:3-4 states, "We were therefore buried with him through baptism into death in order that, just as Christ was raised from the dead through the glory of the Father, we too may live a new life."

Gift of the Holy Spirit: In the book of Acts, Baptism is often followed by the laying on of hands and the reception of the Holy Spirit. This signifies that through Baptism, believers receive the indwelling presence of the Holy Spirit.

The New Covenant in Christianity:

The concept of the New Covenant is closely related to Baptism. In Christian theology, the New Covenant is the promise made by God to humanity through Jesus Christ. It is a central theme in the New Testament and is based on the prophecy found in the Old Testament book of Jeremiah:

"Behold, the days are coming, declares the Lord, when I will make a new covenant with the house of Israel and the house of Judah, not like the covenant that I made with their fathers on the day when I took them by the hand to bring them out of the land of Egypt, my covenant that they broke, though I was their husband, declares the Lord. But this is the covenant that I will make with the house of Israel after those days, declares the Lord: I will put my law within them, and I will write it on their hearts. And I will be their God, and they shall be my people." (Jeremiah 31:31-33)

The New Covenant is seen as a fulfillment of the Old Covenant, which was established through the Mosaic Law and the covenant with Israel at Mount Sinai. The Old Covenant was marked by external laws and sacrifices, while the New Covenant is characterized by an internal transformation of the heart and a relationship with God through faith in Jesus Christ.

Relationship Between Baptism and the New Covenant:

Baptism is closely linked to the New Covenant in several ways:

Covenant Initiation: Baptism is often seen as the ritual of initiation into the New Covenant. Just as circumcision was a sign of the Old Covenant, Baptism is considered the sign of the New Covenant. Through Baptism, a person enters into a new relationship with God based on faith in Christ.

Cleansing and Forgiveness: Baptism symbolizes the forgiveness of sins, which is a key aspect of the New Covenant promise. In the New Covenant, God promises to forgive sins and remember them no more (Hebrews 8:12), and Baptism is the visible representation of this forgiveness.

Regeneration: The concept of being born again, which is associated with Baptism, aligns with the New Covenant promise of God writing His law on the hearts of believers. In the New Covenant, God transforms the hearts of His people, making them new creations in Christ (2 Corinthians 5:17).

Union with Christ: Baptism signifies the believer's union with Christ, and the New Covenant is centered on the relationship between God and His people through Christ. Through Baptism, a person is incorporated into the body of Christ, becoming a part of the covenant community.

Gift of the Holy Spirit: The reception of the Holy Spirit in many Christian traditions is closely associated with Baptism. The presence of the Holy Spirit is a key aspect of the New Covenant, as God promises to indwell His people and empower them for a life of faith and obedience.

It's important to note that the understanding of Baptism and its relationship to the New Covenant can vary among Christian denominations. Some denominations practice infant Baptism, while others emphasize believer's Baptism. The theological significance of Baptism and its connection to the New Covenant may be interpreted differently within these traditions.

Practical Implications of Baptism and the New Covenant:

The theological concepts associated with Baptism and the New Covenant have practical implications for the life of a Christian. Some of these implications include:

Identity and Belonging: Baptism marks an individual's identification with the Christian faith and membership in the body of Christ. It signifies that the person is part of a community of believers who share the same faith and commitment to the New Covenant.

Repentance and Forgiveness: Baptism is often preceded by repentance, a turning away from sin, and a desire for forgiveness. This reflects the core message of the New Covenant, which promises the forgiveness of sins through faith in Christ.

Transformation and Sanctification: Baptism symbolizes a person's commitment to live a new life in Christ. Just as the New Covenant promises a transformed heart and obedience to God's commands, Baptism signifies the believer's desire to live in accordance with God's will.

Empowerment by the Holy Spirit: The gift of the Holy Spirit received in Baptism empowers believers to live out the principles of the New Covenant. The Spirit helps believers grow in faith, love, and obedience to God.

Continual Remembrance: Baptism serves as a continual reminder of the New Covenant and the promises associated with it. It reminds Christians of God's faithfulness and their commitment to follow Him.

In conclusion, Baptism and the New Covenant are deeply interconnected within Christian theology. Baptism is the visible expression of the believer's initiation into the

Covenant Theology

Covenant theology is a significant theological framework that has played a foundational role in various branches of Christian theology. It is a complex and multifaceted system that seeks to understand the relationship between God and humanity throughout history, primarily through the concept of covenants. In this extensive exploration, we will delve into the key elements, historical development, and major tenets of Covenant Theology.

I. Introduction

Covenant theology, often referred to as Reformed theology or Federal theology, is a theological system that has its roots in the Reformation era and has greatly influenced the doctrines of various Protestant traditions. At its core, Covenant Theology seeks to interpret the Bible through the lens of covenants, highlighting the agreements or relationships that God has established with humanity. These covenants serve as the framework for understanding God's plan of salvation and the role of individuals within that plan.

II. Historical Development

Covenant theology has its origins in the writings and teachings of theologians from the 16th and 17th centuries, particularly within the Reformed tradition. The development of this theological system can be traced back to key figures such as John Calvin, Johannes Oecolampadius, Zacharias Ursinus, and Caspar Olevianus. However, it was primarily through the works of John Calvin that the concept of covenant began to take shape as a theological framework.

A. John Calvin

John Calvin, a prominent figure in the Reformation, laid the groundwork for covenant theology in his writings. Although Calvin did not explicitly develop a comprehensive covenant theology, his teachings on God's covenantal relationships with humanity served as a foundation for later theologians to build upon. He emphasized the idea of a covenant of grace, whereby God freely offers salvation to His chosen people through faith.

B. The Westminster Confession of Faith

One of the most influential documents in the development of Covenant Theology is the Westminster Confession of Faith, which was written in the mid-17th century. The Westminster Confession, alongside the Larger and Shorter Catechisms, provides a systematic and detailed exposition of Reformed theology. It articulates the Reformed understanding of covenant theology, particularly the Covenant of Works and the Covenant of Grace.

C. Development of Covenant Theology

Theologians in the Reformed tradition, such as Francis Turretin, Johannes Cocceius, and Herman Witsius, further developed and systematized covenant theology. They expanded on the concepts of the covenants, their nature, and their significance in the context of God's plan of redemption. Covenant theology became a distinct theological system during this period.

III. Key Covenant Concepts

Covenant theology is centered around several key covenant concepts, each of which plays a critical role in shaping the system's theological framework:

A. Covenant of Works

The Covenant of Works is believed to have been established in the Garden of Eden with Adam as the federal head of humanity. In this covenant, God promised life and blessings for perfect obedience and threatened death for disobedience. This concept emphasizes the idea that humanity's sin, as exemplified by Adam's fall, necessitates redemption through the Covenant of Grace.

B. Covenant of Grace

The Covenant of Grace is central to Covenant Theology and is seen as the means by which God provides salvation to fallen humanity. This covenant is based on God's promise of grace, offered freely to those whom He has chosen. It is often associated with the work of Christ on the cross and the application of His redemptive work to believers through faith.

C. Covenant of Redemption

The Covenant of Redemption is a covenant made within the Godhead, where the Father, Son, and Holy Spirit covenanted together to accomplish the redemption of God's elect. The Father sent the Son to fulfill the Covenant of Works on behalf of humanity, and the Spirit applies the benefits of redemption to believers.

D. Covenant of Noah

The Covenant of Noah is described in Genesis 9, following the flood. It is seen as a covenant of preservation, where God promised never again to destroy the world by a flood. This covenant has universal implications and is considered a continuation of the Covenant of Grace.

E. Covenant with Abraham

The Covenant with Abraham is a crucial element in Covenant Theology. God made a covenant with Abraham, promising to bless him and his descendants, who would become a great nation. This covenant is often understood as a precursor to the Covenant of Grace and is fulfilled in Christ.

F. Covenant at Sinai (Mosaic Covenant)

The covenant at Sinai, commonly referred to as the Mosaic Covenant, was made between God and the nation of Israel through Moses. It included the giving of the Ten Commandments and the law. While it is a significant part of biblical history, Covenant Theology sees the Mosaic Covenant as subservient to the Covenant of Grace, serving as a schoolmaster to lead people to Christ.

G. New Covenant

The New Covenant, prophesied in the Old Testament (Jeremiah 31:31-34), is a central focus of Covenant Theology. It is seen as the fulfillment of the Covenant of Grace in Christ. The New Covenant promises forgiveness of sins, the indwelling of the Holy Spirit, and an intimate relationship with God for all who believe in Christ.

IV. Covenant Theology and Eschatology

Covenant theology also plays a significant role in shaping eschatological beliefs, which concern the end times and the final destiny of humanity. The understanding of covenants, particularly the New Covenant, influences how Covenant Theology interprets prophetic passages and the ultimate consummation of God's plan.

A. Amillennialism

Many proponents of Covenant Theology hold to an amillennial eschatology. Amillennialists interpret the book of Revelation and other prophetic texts symbolically, viewing the church age as the fulfillment of God's promises in the New Covenant. They do not expect a literal thousand-year reign of Christ on Earth but anticipate the ultimate return of Christ and the final judgment.

B. Postmillennialism

Some Covenant Theologians adhere to postmillennialism, a view that suggests that the world will gradually become more Christianized through the spread of the gospel and the influence of the church. This will culminate in a golden age of peace and righteousness before Christ's return. Postmillennialism is often associated with optimistic views of human progress and cultural transformation.

C. Dispensationalism

Covenant theology stands in contrast to dispensationalism, another prominent theological framework, especially in the United States. Dispensationalists interpret Scripture more literally and see a clear distinction between Israel and the church. They expect a future, literal fulfillment of many Old Testament prophecies concerning Israel and a distinct seven-year period of tribulation.

V. Criticisms and Controversies

Covenant theology is not without its criticisms and controversies, and various theological traditions have developed alternative perspectives in response to this system.

A. Dispensationalist Critiques

Dispensationalists criticize Covenant Theology for what they see as an allegorical interpretation of biblical prophecy. They argue that Covenant Theology spiritualizes Old Testament promises to Israel and replaces Israel with the church in God's plan, whereas dispensationalism maintains a more literal interpretation and a future role for Israel.

B. New Covenant Theology

New Covenant Theology, as a theological system, emerged as a response to some of the perceived shortcomings of Covenant Theology. Advocates of New Covenant Theology

Symbolism and Meaning

Baptism is a significant religious ritual in many faith traditions, including Christianity, where it holds a central place in the life of believers. This rite involves the use of water, either through immersion, sprinkling, or pouring, and carries deep symbolism and meaning. In this discussion, we will explore the rich tapestry of symbolism and meaning associated with baptism, delving into its historical, theological, and cultural dimensions.

1. Historical Context of Baptism:

Baptism has ancient roots, and its origins can be traced back to various practices in different cultures. In Judaism, the act of ritual purification through water was a common practice, and it is believed to have influenced the development of Christian baptism. Early Christian baptism borrowed elements from Jewish purification rites and the immersion in the River Jordan by John the Baptist, a central figure in Christian history.

2. Christian Sacrament:

BAPTISM A BIBLICAL EXPLORATION

In Christianity, baptism is considered one of the seven sacraments (in Catholicism and Orthodoxy) or as a significant ordinance (in Protestant denominations). It is often referred to as the "sacrament of initiation" because it marks the beginning of one's Christian journey. Baptism is the act by which individuals become part of the Christian community and are initiated into the body of Christ.

3. Water Symbolism:

Water is the central element of baptism, and its symbolism is multifaceted. Water represents purification, cleansing, and rebirth. It signifies the washing away of sins and the start of a new life in Christ. The act of immersion or sprinkling with water symbolizes a spiritual cleansing, much like physical cleanliness.

4. Death and Resurrection:

One of the most profound symbols associated with baptism is the idea of death and resurrection. As the individual is immersed in water and then brought out, it symbolizes dying to the old self, with its sins and imperfections, and rising to a new life in Christ. This concept is deeply rooted in the Christian belief in the resurrection of Jesus Christ, and it represents a spiritual rebirth.

5. Regeneration and Renewal:

Baptism is seen as a moment of regeneration and renewal. It is a transformative experience where a person is "born again" in a spiritual sense. This renewal signifies a break from a life of sin and a commitment to live according to Christian principles and values.

6. Adoption as Children of God:

Baptism is often described as the act of adoption into the family of God. In this context, those who are baptized become children of God, with all the rights and privileges associated with this status. They are seen as heirs to God's promises and recipients of His grace.

7. The Holy Trinity:

In many Christian traditions, baptism is done in the name of the Father, the Son, and the Holy Spirit. This invokes the doctrine of the

Holy Trinity, which is central to Christian theology. The use of the Trinitarian formula in baptism emphasizes the belief in one God in three persons and signifies the involvement of the entire Godhead in the baptismal act.

8. Community and Fellowship:

Baptism is not just an individual act; it is also a communal one. It signifies entry into the community of believers. This sense of community and fellowship is crucial in Christianity, as it fosters a sense of belonging and mutual support among believers.

9. Clothing Symbolism:

In some Christian traditions, a white garment is given to the baptized person. This white robe symbolizes the purity and righteousness that come with the forgiveness of sins through Christ. It is a visible representation of the new life and the new identity in Christ.

10. Anointing with Oil:

In some Christian traditions, anointing with oil is part of the baptismal ritual. Oil is often associated with the Holy Spirit and is seen as a symbol of empowerment and consecration for a life of faith and service.

11. Entry into the Church:

Baptism is the gateway to participation in the life of the Church. It marks the beginning of a Christian's involvement in the various activities and ministries of the Church, including the reception of other sacraments like the Eucharist (Holy Communion).

12. Faith and Repentance:

Baptism is closely linked to faith and repentance. It is an expression of one's faith in Christ as Lord and Savior and a commitment to turn away from sin. In this sense, baptism is a public declaration of one's beliefs and intentions.

13. A Seal of the Covenant:

In some Christian traditions, baptism is considered a seal of God's covenant with His people. It is a tangible sign of God's promises and

His commitment to be with His people throughout their journey of faith.

14. The Great Commission:

For many Christians, the practice of baptism is grounded in the Great Commission given by Jesus in the New Testament. In the Gospel of Matthew (Matthew 28:18-20), Jesus instructs his disciples to baptize in the name of the Father, Son, and Holy Spirit, making disciples of all nations. This commission emphasizes the universal and missionary aspect of baptism.

15. Symbol of Evangelism:

Baptism can serve as a powerful symbol of evangelism. When someone witnesses a baptism, it can be an opportunity for evangelism, as it presents a visual and experiential representation of the Gospel message. It can inspire others to consider their own faith journey.

16. Various Christian Denominations:

It's important to note that the symbolism and meaning of baptism can vary among different Christian denominations. While the core elements of water, purification, and rebirth are consistent, there may be variations in the mode of baptism (immersion, sprinkling, pouring), the age at which it is administered (infant baptism, believer's baptism), and the theological emphasis placed on certain aspects of the rite.

17. Infant Baptism vs. Believer's Baptism:

The theological differences between infant baptism and believer's baptism highlight the diversity within Christianity. In infant baptism, the emphasis is on God's grace and the covenantal relationship between God and the child, with the expectation that the child will later confirm their faith. In believer's baptism, the emphasis is on a personal confession of faith before baptism, often by immersion.

18. Ecumenical Significance:

Baptism holds ecumenical significance as a unifying symbol among various Christian traditions. While there are theological differences, the shared recognition of baptism as a central Christian rite serves as a point of unity among many denominations and a testament to the common faith in Jesus Christ.

19. Cultural and Regional Variations:

Baptism also takes on cultural and regional variations, with different traditions and customs associated with the rite. These variations reflect the adaptability of baptism to local customs and practices while retaining its core symbolism.

20. Continual Renewal:

Baptism is not a one-time event but symbolizes a continual process of renewal and growth in the Christian faith. It reminds believers of their ongoing need for spiritual cleansing and transformation throughout their lives.

In conclusion, the symbolism and meaning of baptism in Christianity are profound and multi-dimensional. It encompasses themes of purification, regeneration, community, and identity in Christ. Baptism is a central act of faith that signifies the beginning of a Christian journey and the believer's commitment to a life of discipleship. Its rich historical and theological roots, along with its cultural and denominational

Connection to the Lord's Supper

The connection between baptism and the Lord's Supper is a subject of significant theological discussion and debate within the Christian faith. These two sacraments, or ordinances, hold a central place in various Christian traditions, but their specific relationship and significance can vary. In this extended discussion, I will elaborate on the connection between baptism and the Lord's Supper, their individual meanings, historical development, and how different Christian denominations interpret and practice them.

Baptism: A Sacrament of Initiation

Baptism is one of the foundational sacraments in Christianity, signifying the initiation of a person into the faith. The act of baptism involves the use of water, typically through immersion, pouring, or sprinkling, and the pronouncement of words or blessings by a minister or priest. While the mode and specific liturgical practices can vary among Christian denominations, the core symbolism remains constant: baptism is a symbol of spiritual cleansing, regeneration, and entry into the community of believers.

Historical and Scriptural Background

The practice of baptism has deep roots in the Christian tradition, and its origins can be traced back to the teachings and actions of Jesus Christ and the early Christian community. In the New Testament, we find references to baptism in the Gospels and the writings of the apostles. For example, in the Gospel of Matthew, Jesus instructs his disciples to "Go therefore and make disciples of all nations, baptizing them in the name of the Father and of the Son and of the Holy Spirit" (Matthew 28:19). This Great Commission is often cited as a scriptural basis for Christian baptism.

In the book of Acts, we see numerous accounts of individuals being baptized upon their conversion to Christianity. The most famous of these accounts is the baptism of the Ethiopian eunuch by Philip (Acts 8:26-39). These scriptural references serve as a foundation for the practice of baptism in Christian theology.

Theological Significance

Theological interpretations of baptism vary among Christian denominations, but several common themes can be identified:

Cleansing and Forgiveness: Baptism is seen as a means of washing away sin and receiving forgiveness. This concept is rooted in the idea that baptism connects the believer with the redemptive work of Jesus Christ, who offered himself as a sacrifice for the forgiveness of sins.

Regeneration and New Birth: Baptism symbolizes a spiritual rebirth or regeneration. It represents a transition from a state of spiritual death to a new life in Christ. This concept is often expressed with the metaphor of being "born again."

Incorporation into the Church: Baptism is viewed as the rite of initiation into the community of believers, the universal Church. It signifies the believer's commitment to follow Christ and participate in the life of the Church.

Reception of the Holy Spirit: In some Christian traditions, baptism is associated with the reception of the Holy Spirit. This is particularly emphasized in Pentecostal and Charismatic denominations, where the "baptism of the Holy Spirit" is a distinct experience subsequent to water baptism.

The Lord's Supper: A Sacrament of Commemoration

The Lord's Supper, also known as the Eucharist or Holy Communion, is another central sacrament in Christianity. It is a commemorative ritual that recalls the Last Supper of Jesus with his disciples on the night before his crucifixion. The key elements of the Lord's Supper are bread and wine (or grape juice), which are consecrated and shared among the participants. This sacrament holds a significant place in Christian worship, and its interpretation and practice can vary among denominations.

Historical and Scriptural Background

The origins of the Lord's Supper are rooted in the accounts of the Last Supper as recorded in the Gospels, particularly in the synoptic Gospels of Matthew, Mark, and Luke. In these accounts, Jesus takes bread, blesses it, breaks it, and gives it to his disciples, saying, "This is my body." He then takes a cup of wine, blesses it, and shares it with them, saying, "This is my blood of the covenant, which is poured out for many" (Mark 14:22-24).

The apostle Paul also provides significant theological insights into the Lord's Supper in his first letter to the Corinthians (1 Corinthians 11:23-26). In this passage, he emphasizes the importance of partaking in a worthy manner, discerning the body of Christ, and proclaiming the Lord's death until he comes.

Theological Significance

Theological interpretations of the Lord's Supper vary, but several common themes can be identified:

Remembrance and Commemoration: The Lord's Supper is primarily a commemorative act. It serves as a way for Christians to remember and celebrate the sacrificial death and resurrection of Jesus Christ. It is a solemn occasion that calls believers to reflect on the significance of Christ's atonement for their sins.

Real Presence: One of the most debated aspects of the Lord's Supper is the concept of the "real presence" of Christ in the elements. Different traditions interpret this differently, with some believing in a literal transformation of the bread and wine into the body and blood of Christ (transubstantiation), while others see it as a symbolic or spiritual presence (consubstantiation or memorialism).

Fellowship and Unity: The act of partaking in the Lord's Supper is often seen as a communal and unifying experience. It emphasizes the idea that all believers are one body in Christ, regardless of denominational differences. It also underscores the importance of reconciliation and forgiveness among believers.

Anticipation of the Kingdom: The Lord's Supper is viewed by many Christians as a foretaste of the heavenly banquet that will be enjoyed in the future kingdom of God. It is a symbol of hope and anticipation for the ultimate fulfillment of God's purposes.

The Connection Between Baptism and the Lord's Supper

The relationship between baptism and the Lord's Supper has been a subject of theological reflection and debate throughout Christian history. While both are considered sacraments and play crucial roles in the life of the Church, their connections are nuanced and interpreted differently by various Christian traditions.

Common Elements

There are several common elements that connect baptism and the Lord's Supper:

Initiation and Continuation: Baptism is often seen as the initiation into the Christian faith, while the Lord's Supper is viewed as a continuation of the Christian journey. Together, they mark the entrance into and ongoing participation in the life of the Church.

Connection to Christ's Work: Both sacraments are linked to the redemptive work of Christ. Baptism signifies the forgiveness of sins and regeneration through Christ's sacrifice, while the Lord's Supper commemorates his sacrificial death and resurrection.

Incorporation into the Body of Christ: Baptism is the rite of initiation into the Christian community, and the Lord's Supper is a communal act that reinforces the idea of believers as one body in Christ. Together, they emphasize the importance of Christian fellowship and unity.

Sacramental Nature: Baptism and the Lord's Supper are both considered sacraments by most Christian denominations. They are physical and visible signs that convey spiritual realities. These sacraments serve as means of grace through which God communicates with believers.

Chapter 5: The Mode of Baptism

Baptism is a significant religious ritual observed by various Christian denominations, symbolizing purification, initiation, and the incorporation of individuals into the faith. One of the key debates surrounding baptism revolves around the mode or method of its administration. Different Christian traditions adhere to distinct modes of baptism, each with its theological significance and historical roots.

One of the primary modes of baptism is immersion, where the individual is fully submerged in water. This practice traces its origins to the early Christian Church and the baptism of Jesus by John the Baptist in the Jordan River. Proponents of immersion argue that it closely aligns with the symbolic meaning of baptism, representing death to sin and resurrection to a new life in Christ.

On the other hand, affusion, or pouring water over the head, is another prevalent mode of baptism. This method gained popularity over the centuries, especially in regions where access to large bodies of water was limited. Advocates of affusion emphasize its practicality and argue that the mode itself is secondary to the spiritual significance of the sacrament.

A third mode is aspersion, which involves sprinkling water on the individual. This mode is often associated with practical considerations, such as the baptism of infants or individuals with health concerns that may limit immersion or pouring. Some argue that the biblical accounts of baptism may allow for flexibility in the mode used.

The choice of baptismal mode often reflects theological beliefs and traditions within specific Christian denominations. For example, many Baptist and Evangelical churches strongly advocate for immersion, viewing it as the most faithful representation of biblical baptism. Conversely, many Anglican, Lutheran, and Methodist traditions accept various modes, accommodating differences in practice while emphasizing the spiritual meaning of baptism.

Historically, debates over baptismal modes have sometimes led to schisms within Christian communities. The Anabaptist movement, emerging during the 16th century, played a significant role in promoting believer's baptism through immersion. This movement faced opposition from other Christian groups, reflecting the deep theological divides on the issue.

As Christianity spread globally, diverse cultural and regional factors influenced the mode of baptism adopted by different communities. The rich tapestry of Christian traditions encompasses a spectrum of beliefs and practices regarding baptism, creating a vibrant and diverse landscape within the larger faith.

In conclusion, the mode of baptism is a nuanced and multifaceted aspect of Christian theology and practice. The historical, cultural, and theological dimensions of immersion, affusion, and aspersion contribute to the diversity within the Christian faith. While differences exist among denominations, the common thread uniting them is the recognition of baptism as a sacred and symbolic rite, regardless of the mode chosen.

Immersion, Pouring, or Sprinkling

Immersion, pouring, and sprinkling each evoke distinct sensory experiences. Immersion engulfs, a complete submersion in an experience that wraps around you like a comforting blanket. It's diving headfirst into a world, whether it's a captivating story, a new culture, or even the warmth of a hot bath at the end of a long day. Immersion demands your full attention, a surrender to the depths of the moment.

Pouring, on the other hand, carries a sense of intentionality. It's a deliberate act, the steady stream of focus directed toward a specific purpose. Like pouring liquid into a container, it's about the controlled release of energy or effort. Pouring yourself into a project, a relationship, or a passion implies a gradual and purposeful investment, allowing the substance to spread and fill the contours of its surroundings.

Sprinkling introduces an element of playfulness. It's the light touch, the subtle enhancement that adds a dash of flavor to life. Sprinkling is like the gentle rain that falls on a summer day, refreshing and leaving a subtle imprint. It's the small gestures, the moments of joy or kindness that, when scattered throughout life, create a mosaic of meaningful experiences. Sprinkling invites spontaneity, embracing the beauty in the details.

In essence, immersion, pouring, and sprinkling offer varied approaches to engagement. Immersion provides depth and saturation, pouring offers intentionality and directed effort, while sprinkling brings a touch of whimsy and lightness. Depending on the context, each method can enhance the richness of our experiences, creating a nuanced tapestry of life.

Historical Practice

Baptism, a ritual with deep historical roots, has evolved over centuries within various cultures and religious traditions. The practice of baptism has taken on diverse forms, meanings, and significance throughout history, shaping the spiritual landscape of numerous societies.

One of the earliest recorded instances of baptism can be traced back to ancient civilizations, where water rituals were employed as symbols of purification and spiritual cleansing. In ancient Egypt, for example, individuals underwent ritualistic immersions in the Nile River to symbolize the washing away of impurities and sins. Similarly, in Hinduism, the practice of ablution in the sacred river Ganges carries profound spiritual significance, reflecting the desire for spiritual renewal and the removal of sins.

The roots of baptism also extend into Judaism, where ritual immersion, known as mikveh, holds a central place in purification ceremonies. This practice influenced early Christian baptism, as Jesus himself underwent baptism in the Jordan River by John the Baptist, setting a pivotal example for his followers.

Christian baptism, as it is widely recognized today, emerged as a sacrament within the early Christian communities. The New Testament documents, particularly the Gospels and the Acts of the Apostles, provide accounts of baptisms administered by John the Baptist and later by the apostles. The act of baptism symbolized not only the repentance of sins but also the initiation into the Christian faith.

Throughout the early centuries of Christianity, variations in baptismal practices arose among different Christian communities. The modes of administration (such as immersion, pouring, or sprinkling), the age at which baptism was performed, and the theological understanding of baptism diverged among various Christian denominations. Theologians like Augustine and Thomas Aquinas contributed to the theological discourse surrounding baptism, addressing issues such as original sin and the transformative nature of the sacrament.

The Great Schism of 1054 marked a significant turning point in the history of Christianity, leading to the separation of the Western (Roman Catholic) and Eastern (Eastern Orthodox) Churches. Despite this division, both traditions maintained the practice of baptism as a fundamental sacrament, albeit with some variations in liturgical rites and theological nuances.

During the medieval period, baptism became increasingly intertwined with the concept of salvation. The Catholic Church emphasized the role of baptism in the remission of sin and the infusion of divine grace, solidifying its status as a crucial sacrament. This period also witnessed the rise of infant baptism, as the Church emphasized the necessity of baptizing infants to cleanse them of original sin.

The Protestant Reformation in the 16th century brought about further changes to the practice of baptism. Reformers like Martin Luther and John Calvin challenged certain aspects of Catholic baptismal theology, advocating for a return to biblical principles.

Anabaptists, a radical group within the Reformation, rejected infant baptism and promoted the idea of believer's baptism, arguing that individuals should be baptized only upon a conscious profession of faith.

The subsequent centuries saw the global spread of Christianity through colonialism and missionary endeavors, leading to the adaptation of baptismal practices in diverse cultural contexts. Different Christian denominations developed unique liturgical rites and ceremonies, incorporating elements of local traditions into the sacrament of baptism.

In the modern era, ecumenical efforts have aimed to foster greater unity among Christian denominations, including a shared understanding of baptism. The Second Vatican Council (1962-1965) in the Catholic Church, for instance, sought to promote ecumenism and emphasized the importance of baptism as a common bond among Christians.

Today, baptism remains a significant rite of passage for Christians worldwide, symbolizing entry into the community of believers and the forgiveness of sins. While variations persist in the modes and theological interpretations of baptism, the practice continues to be a central and unifying element within the diverse tapestry of Christian traditions.

Historical practices of immersion, pouring, and sprinkling have deep roots in various cultures and religions. Immersion, often associated with baptism, has been a significant ritual in Christianity, symbolizing purification and rebirth. The act of being fully submerged in water signifies a cleansing of sins and a spiritual renewal.

Pouring, another method of baptism, involves gently pouring water over the individual's head. This practice has been prevalent in Christian denominations that view the symbolic act of pouring as a representation of the Holy Spirit descending upon the person. It emphasizes the transformative power of divine grace.

Sprinkling, also known as affusion, is a method where water is lightly sprinkled or poured on an individual. This practice has historical roots in various religious traditions, including Judaism and Christianity. In Judaism, sprinkling is associated with purification rituals, while in some Christian denominations, it serves as a form of baptism.

In ancient times, immersion had diverse cultural significance beyond religious contexts. In ancient Greek and Roman cultures, immersion was part of various purification rituals associated with different gods and goddesses. The practice symbolized the cleansing of both the body and the soul.

The historical practice of immersion extends beyond Christianity and ancient civilizations. In Hinduism, the ritual of immersion is a crucial aspect of the Kumbh Mela festival, where millions of devotees gather to bathe in the sacred rivers. This act is believed to cleanse individuals of their sins and grant them spiritual merit.

Pouring and sprinkling rituals have also found their place in diverse cultural and religious practices. In Japanese Shinto ceremonies, purification rites involve the use of water, either poured or sprinkled, to cleanse participants and sacred objects. Similarly, in African traditional religions, pouring libations is a common practice to honor ancestors and seek their guidance.

Throughout history, these water-based rituals have been adapted and incorporated into various belief systems, each with its unique symbolism and significance. The choice between immersion, pouring, or sprinkling often reflects theological interpretations and cultural preferences within religious communities.

As societies evolved, so did the interpretations and practices associated with immersion, pouring, and sprinkling. The Reformation era in Christianity, for instance, saw debates over the mode of baptism, with some denominations favoring immersion while others embraced pouring or sprinkling. These debates often reflected theological nuances and differing views on the symbolism behind each method.

In modern times, the choice between immersion, pouring, or sprinkling remains a subject of discussion and variation within religious communities. Denominations may adhere to specific practices based on their interpretation of religious texts and traditions. Interfaith dialogue has also led to increased awareness and understanding of the diverse ways in which these rituals are approached across different religions.

In conclusion, the historical practices of immersion, pouring, and sprinkling have rich and varied histories, rooted in cultural, religious, and social contexts. These rituals continue to be significant aspects of ceremonies and celebrations, serving as symbols of purification, rebirth, and spiritual transformation across different faith traditions.

Theological Implications

Theological discussions surrounding baptism methods often center on immersion, sprinkling, and pouring. Immersion, where a person is fully submerged in water, is seen by some as a symbolic representation of death, burial, and resurrection, aligning with Christian beliefs. It reflects the cleansing of sin and rebirth.

On the other hand, sprinkling, known as affusion, is rooted in historical practices and is associated with purification. It draws parallels to Old Testament rituals, where sprinkling was used for ceremonial cleansing. Some argue that it symbolizes the outpouring of the Holy Spirit.

Pouring, or infusion, involves pouring water over the individual's head, symbolizing the Holy Spirit's descent. This method is often linked to theological views emphasizing God's grace rather than human action. It underscores the idea that God's grace is poured out upon believers.

Theological debates arise regarding the validity and significance of each method. Immersion advocates emphasize biblical examples, such as Jesus' baptism in the Jordan River. Sprinkling supporters refer to Old Testament practices and argue for the continuity of symbolism. Pouring proponents highlight the symbolism of the Holy Spirit's descent and the emphasis on divine action.

Denominational differences further contribute to these discussions, with some traditions strongly favoring one method over others. Ultimately, these theological implications reflect diverse perspectives on the sacrament of baptism and its profound spiritual meaning within Christian faith.

Chapter 6: Infant Baptism

Infant baptism, also known as pediatric baptism, is a religious practice that has been a subject of theological discussion and debate within various Christian denominations. The ritual involves the administration of the sacrament of baptism to infants or young children, typically within the first few months of their lives. This practice is rooted in historical, theological, and cultural contexts, and its significance varies among different Christian traditions.

One of the key theological foundations for infant baptism can be traced back to the concept of covenant theology. In many Christian denominations, believers view the covenant between God and humanity as continuous, starting with the Old Testament and continuing into the New Testament. The covenantal relationship is seen as including not only adults but also their children. This perspective draws parallels between circumcision in the Old Testament and baptism in the New Testament, considering them as signs of initiation into God's covenant community.

Another theological argument supporting infant baptism is the belief in original sin. According to this doctrine, humans are born with a sinful nature inherited from the first human, Adam. Baptism is seen as a means of grace that cleanses individuals, including infants, from this inherited sin and initiates them into the faith community. The sacrament is perceived as a transformative act, symbolizing the washing away of sin and the regeneration of the baptized individual.

Historically, infant baptism can be traced back to the early centuries of Christianity. Early Christian writings, such as the "Didache," suggest that the practice was already established in the first-century Christian community. The emergence of infant baptism can be linked to the understanding of baptism as a means of salvation and the desire to ensure the salvation of infants who were vulnerable to illness or death.

However, it's essential to note that not all Christian denominations practice infant baptism. Some denominations, including Baptists and many Evangelical groups, adhere to believer's baptism, which emphasizes a personal profession of faith before undergoing the sacrament. In this view, baptism is reserved for those who can consciously choose to follow Christ and understand the significance of the ritual.

The mode of baptism also varies among denominations practicing infant baptism. While some traditions practice sprinkling or pouring of water, others practice immersion, wherein the infant is fully submerged in water. The mode of baptism is often influenced by theological beliefs and historical practices within specific denominations.

The debate over infant baptism extends beyond theology to encompass cultural, social, and familial considerations. In some communities, infant baptism is not only a religious ceremony but also a cultural tradition and a rite of passage. Families may choose to baptize their infants as a way of expressing their religious identity and connecting with their faith community.

In conclusion, infant baptism is a multifaceted practice with theological, historical, and cultural dimensions. Its acceptance or rejection depends on the doctrinal beliefs and traditions of each Christian denomination. The debate surrounding infant baptism reflects the diversity within Christianity and the nuanced perspectives on the nature and purpose of the sacrament.

Historical Development

Baptism has a rich historical development that spans centuries and is deeply rooted in religious and cultural practices. The origins of baptism can be traced back to various ancient civilizations, where ritualistic purification ceremonies were common. In this extensive exploration, we'll delve into key milestones and shifts in the historical development of baptism.

Ancient Rituals:

The concept of ritualistic cleansing is evident in the religious practices of ancient civilizations. In Mesopotamia, for instance, the Epic of Gilgamesh describes a purification ritual in the river Euphrates. Similarly, ancient Egyptians practiced ritual bathing for spiritual purification.

Jewish Mikvah:

The Jewish tradition significantly influenced the development of baptism. The Mikvah, a ritual bath used for immersion, became a symbol of spiritual cleansing in Judaism. Ritual immersion was a key element in Jewish purification practices, notably in the context of conversion and repentance.

John the Baptist:

A pivotal figure in the history of baptism is John the Baptist, a Jewish preacher mentioned in the Gospels. He is often credited with baptizing Jesus in the Jordan River, marking a significant shift in the purpose and symbolism of baptism. John's baptism was seen as a ritual of repentance and preparation for the coming Messiah.

Early Christian Practices:

The early Christian community adopted and adapted baptism from Jewish traditions. Baptism became a central rite symbolizing initiation into the Christian faith. The New Testament contains references to baptism, emphasizing its role in forgiveness of sins and new spiritual birth.

Emergence of Formulas:

As Christianity spread, various Christian communities developed distinct baptismal formulas and practices. The Didache, an early Christian document, provides insights into baptismal practices, emphasizing the importance of immersion in living water or cold running water. Different regions and sects had variations in the administration of the sacrament.

Constantine and Christianization:

The conversion of Emperor Constantine to Christianity in the 4th century had a profound impact on the historical development of baptism. Christianity became a state religion, leading to increased standardization of religious practices, including baptism. Baptismal fonts in churches became common, and infant baptism gained acceptance.

Medieval Period:

During the medieval period, baptism continued to evolve. The theological understanding of baptism became more refined, with debates on issues such as the nature of original sin and the age of candidates for baptism. The sacrament became more formalized within the Christian liturgy.

Protestant Reformation:

The Protestant Reformation in the 16th century brought about significant changes in Christian theology and practice, including baptism. Martin Luther and other reformers emphasized the primacy of faith in salvation, impacting the understanding of baptism. While infant baptism remained common, the mode and significance of the sacrament varied among Protestant denominations.

Modern Denominational Variances:

In contemporary times, different Christian denominations maintain diverse practices regarding baptism. Some emphasize believer's baptism, associating it with a personal confession of faith, while others practice infant baptism, viewing it as a covenantal sign. The mode of baptism (immersion, pouring, or sprinkling) also varies among denominations.

Ecumenical Dialogues:

In recent decades, ecumenical dialogues among Christian denominations have aimed at finding common ground on theological issues, including baptism. Agreements have been reached on the mutual recognition of baptisms performed in various Christian traditions.

Conclusion:

The historical development of baptism is a fascinating journey that intertwines with the evolution of religious beliefs, cultural practices, and theological understandings. From ancient purification rituals to the diverse practices in contemporary Christianity, baptism has played a central role in shaping the spiritual identity of individuals and communities throughout history.

Scriptural Support and Critiques

Baptism holds a significant place in Christian theology, symbolizing spiritual purification and initiation into the faith. One key scriptural reference is found in the New Testament, specifically in Matthew 28:19-20, where Jesus instructs his disciples to baptize in the name of the Father, the Son, and the Holy Spirit. This passage is often referred to as the Great Commission, emphasizing the importance of baptism as a central practice for believers.

Another crucial biblical account is the baptism of Jesus by John the Baptist, described in Matthew 3:13-17, Mark 1:9-11, Luke 3:21-22, and John 1:29-34. This event marks the beginning of Jesus' public ministry and exemplifies the symbolic nature of baptism. Jesus' baptism signifies his identification with humanity and sets an example for his followers.

The Apostle Paul, in his letters to various early Christian communities, further elaborates on the theological significance of baptism. Romans 6:3-4 emphasizes the union of believers with Christ through baptism, depicting it as a symbolic burial and resurrection. Colossians 2:12 connects baptism with spiritual circumcision, highlighting the removal of sin through faith in Christ.

However, it's crucial to acknowledge differing interpretations and critiques of baptism within Christianity. Some denominations, like Baptists, emphasize believer's baptism, asserting that individuals should be baptized only after a personal profession of faith. This perspective is rooted in the idea that baptism is a public declaration of one's commitment to Christ.

On the other hand, infant baptism is practiced by various Christian traditions, including Catholicism and Orthodox Christianity. Advocates argue that it signifies God's grace and covenant relationship with believers from infancy. Prominent passages used to support this view include Acts 2:38-39, where Peter mentions the promise of the Holy Spirit for both adults and their children.

Critics of infant baptism argue that it lacks scriptural precedent and undermines the notion of a conscious, personal decision to follow Christ. They often point to examples of adult baptisms in the New Testament, such as the Ethiopian eunuch (Acts 8:36-39) and the Philippian jailer (Acts 16:25-34).

In conclusion, baptism is a multifaceted topic within Christianity, with scriptural support and varying interpretations. While certain passages highlight its symbolic significance and mandate for believers, different denominations approach the practice with nuanced perspectives, leading to ongoing theological discussions within the Christian community.

Theology of Infant Baptism

Infant baptism is a theological topic that has sparked extensive debate and discussion within Christian traditions. Proponents argue that it symbolizes the child's inclusion into the covenant community and emphasizes the role of God's grace in salvation. On the other hand, opponents often raise concerns about the child's inability to make a conscious decision of faith.

The theological foundation of infant baptism can be traced back to various biblical interpretations. Advocates often point to passages like Acts 2:38-39, where Peter declares that the promise of the Holy Spirit is for both adults and their children. Additionally, they may reference instances of household baptisms in the New Testament, such as the baptism of Lydia and her household in Acts 16:15.

BAPTISM A BIBLICAL EXPLORATION

One key theological perspective supporting infant baptism is the covenantal view. This perspective emphasizes God's covenant relationships with humanity throughout biblical history. Advocates argue that, just as circumcision was a sign of the Abrahamic covenant in the Old Testament, infant baptism serves as a parallel sign in the New Testament era.

Furthermore, proponents of infant baptism often highlight the concept of God's prevenient grace. This notion suggests that God's grace is at work in individuals even before they are capable of understanding or responding to it. In the case of infants, baptism becomes a visible expression of God's initiating love and grace, marking them as members of the faith community.

Conversely, opponents of infant baptism often adhere to a believer's baptism perspective, asserting that baptism should follow a conscious decision of faith. This view draws inspiration from passages like Acts 8:12, where it is stated that both men and women believed and were baptized.

Another theological concern raised by opponents is the potential distortion of the sacrament's significance. They argue that infant baptism may risk diluting the profound symbolism of a believer's conscious identification with Christ's death, burial, and resurrection.

Amidst these theological debates, it's essential to recognize the diversity of views within Christian denominations. While some denominations, such as Roman Catholicism and many mainstream Protestant traditions, practice infant baptism, others, like Baptists and certain evangelical groups, adhere strictly to believer's baptism.

In conclusion, the theology of infant baptism is a complex and nuanced topic that involves careful examination of biblical passages, historical practices, and theological frameworks. Ultimately, individuals and communities navigate this theological landscape guided by their interpretation of Scripture and the traditions within which they find themselves.

Chapter 7: Baptism and Christian Living

Baptism, a sacred rite in Christianity, holds profound significance in the life of a believer. Rooted in biblical tradition, it symbolizes purification, rebirth, and initiation into the Christian faith. The act of baptism is multifaceted, encompassing various theological, symbolic, and practical dimensions that shape the spiritual journey of individuals within the Christian community.

At its core, baptism is a symbolic representation of cleansing and renewal. Drawing inspiration from biblical narratives, particularly the baptism of Jesus by John the Baptist in the River Jordan, Christians view baptism as a transformative experience. The immersion in water symbolizes the washing away of sins and the emergence from the water signifies a new life in Christ. This ritual serves as a powerful expression of faith, as believers publicly declare their commitment to follow the teachings of Jesus and embrace the Christian way of life.

The theological underpinnings of baptism are deeply rooted in Christian doctrine. Different denominations may interpret the sacrament with varying emphasis on its salvific nature, but common threads include the acknowledgment of God's grace and the role of faith in the process. For many Christians, baptism is not a mere ritual but a sacrament through which divine grace is mediated to the individual. The theological nuances surrounding baptism often contribute to denominational diversity, with distinctions in beliefs about infant baptism, believer's baptism, and the mode of administration.

Christian living, on the other hand, extends beyond the moment of baptism, encompassing the entire journey of faith. It is a dynamic and ongoing process marked by the intentional application of Christian principles in daily life. The ethical teachings found in the Bible serve as a guide for believers, shaping their attitudes, actions, and relationships.

Love, compassion, forgiveness, and humility are among the virtues emphasized in Christian living, reflecting the teachings of Jesus Christ.

The concept of Christian living is deeply intertwined with the idea of discipleship—a commitment to follow Jesus and model one's life after His example. This involves not only adhering to moral precepts but also cultivating a personal relationship with God through prayer, worship, and the study of scripture. The Christian life is characterized by a continuous journey of spiritual growth, as individuals strive to align their values with those espoused in the Bible.

Community plays a vital role in Christian living, fostering a sense of fellowship and accountability among believers. The early Christian communities, as depicted in the New Testament, exemplify the importance of communal support in navigating the challenges of living a Christian life. Today, churches and Christian organizations provide avenues for believers to connect, share experiences, and collectively live out their faith.

In the contemporary context, Christian living also involves engagement with broader societal issues. Advocacy for justice, compassion for the marginalized, and stewardship of the environment are increasingly recognized as integral components of a holistic Christian life. The call to be salt and light in the world, as articulated by Jesus, motivates believers to actively contribute to the betterment of society while remaining grounded in their faith.

In conclusion, baptism and Christian living are interconnected aspects of the Christian faith, representing initiation and ongoing commitment, respectively. Baptism serves as a symbolic entry into the Christian community, while Christian living encompasses the daily application of faith, guided by ethical principles and a commitment to discipleship. Together, these elements form the foundation for a meaningful and transformative Christian journey.

The Role of Baptism in Discipleship

Baptism holds a significant role in discipleship, serving as a symbolic and transformative rite within Christian traditions. At its core, baptism is a visible expression of one's commitment to following Jesus Christ, marking the initiation into a life of discipleship. This sacred ritual is rooted in both historical and biblical contexts, shaping the understanding and practice of discipleship in various Christian denominations.

In the New Testament, baptism is prominently associated with the ministry of John the Baptist and later embraced by Jesus and his disciples. John's baptism, initially a call to repentance, foreshadowed the transformative nature of the Christian sacrament. When Jesus himself was baptized by John in the Jordan River, it signaled the beginning of his public ministry and set a profound example for his followers.

The theological underpinnings of baptism in discipleship are multifaceted. One key aspect is the symbolism of cleansing and rebirth. Water, the central element of baptism, represents purification and renewal. Through baptism, believers symbolically participate in the death and resurrection of Jesus Christ, shedding their old selves and rising to a new life in Him. This spiritual rebirth aligns with the biblical notion of being "born again" or "born of water and the Spirit" (John 3:3-7).

Furthermore, baptism serves as a public declaration of faith and allegiance to Christ. It is a communal act, witnessed by fellow believers, creating a sense of unity within the body of Christ. This public testimony becomes a foundation for Christian discipleship, as individuals commit to a life of obedience to God's Word and the teachings of Jesus.

The role of baptism extends beyond symbolism, delving into the realm of community and accountability. The act of baptism is not solitary but communal, emphasizing the interconnectedness of believers within the Church. This communal aspect reinforces the idea that discipleship is not an isolated journey but a shared pilgrimage with fellow believers. The Church, as the community of faith, plays a crucial role in nurturing and supporting individuals on their discipleship journey.

Baptism also aligns with the Great Commission, where Jesus instructs his disciples to go and make disciples of all nations, baptizing them in the name of the Father, the Son, and the Holy Spirit (Matthew 28:19-20). This commission highlights the integral connection between baptism and the disciple-making process. Baptism becomes a tangible expression of evangelism and mission, as believers are called to share the transformative message of Christ and invite others to join the community of disciples.

The ongoing significance of baptism in discipleship is evident in the practices of various Christian traditions. While interpretations and modes of baptism may vary—whether by immersion, pouring, or sprinkling—the fundamental essence remains consistent. It is a sacrament that transcends denominational boundaries, emphasizing the foundational principles of faith, repentance, and commitment to a life of discipleship.

In conclusion, the role of baptism in discipleship is rich and multi-layered. From its biblical origins to its symbolic representations, baptism serves as a pivotal moment in the journey of a believer. It encapsulates the themes of cleansing, rebirth, public testimony, community, and mission, weaving together a tapestry that shapes the identity and trajectory of a disciple. As Christians partake in the sacrament of baptism, they not only engage with a historical and biblical legacy but also embrace a transformative process that propels them into a deeper, more committed walk with Christ.

Living out the Baptismal Covenant

Living out the Baptismal Covenant is a profound journey of faith and commitment. At its core, this covenant represents a sacred agreement between an individual and God, grounded in the teachings of Christianity. As one embarks on this spiritual odyssey, they are called to embody the principles encapsulated in the covenant, navigating the intricate tapestry of faith, love, and service.

The covenant comprises promises to affirm one's faith, resist evil, repent of sin, proclaim the Gospel, and seek and serve Christ in all persons. These promises are not mere words but a roadmap for shaping one's life in accordance with Christian values. Affirming faith involves an unwavering dedication to God and the acknowledgment of His divine presence in every aspect of existence.

Resisting evil is a continual struggle against the forces that seek to undermine goodness and compassion. It demands a vigilant heart, discerning between right and wrong, and an unwavering commitment to uphold moral integrity. Repentance, a pivotal aspect of the covenant, underscores the recognition of human fallibility and the continuous journey towards spiritual growth and transformation.

Proclaiming the Gospel is an active endeavor to share the message of Christ's love and salvation with the world. It involves both words and actions, living in a way that reflects the teachings of Jesus and serves as a testament to the transformative power of faith. Seeking and serving Christ in all persons is a call to embody love, empathy, and compassion in our interactions with others, recognizing the divine spark in every individual.

Living out the Baptismal Covenant is not a solitary pursuit but a communal endeavor. The Christian community provides support, guidance, and a shared sense of purpose. Together, believers strive to create a community that mirrors the principles of the covenant, fostering an environment where love and justice prevail.

The journey of living out the Baptismal Covenant is marked by both triumphs and challenges. It requires resilience in the face of adversity, humility in moments of pride, and a steadfast commitment to the ideals espoused in the covenant. The Christian life is not exempt from hardships, but it is through these trials that faith is refined and deepened.

Prayer becomes an essential companion on this journey, a channel through which individuals communicate with God, seek guidance, and find solace. It is in the moments of prayer that the covenant comes alive, as believers pour out their hearts, expressing gratitude, seeking forgiveness, and renewing their commitment to God.

The sacraments, particularly the Eucharist, hold a central place in living out the Baptismal Covenant. The act of partaking in the body and blood of Christ serves as a tangible reminder of the covenant and a source of spiritual nourishment. It is a sacred moment of communion with God and fellow believers, reinforcing the bonds that unite the Christian community.

Living out the Baptismal Covenant also extends beyond the walls of the church into the broader community and world. Social justice and advocacy become integral components of the Christian life, as believers strive to address systemic inequalities, alleviate suffering, and contribute to the betterment of society. The covenant calls for active engagement in the world, transforming faith into action.

In conclusion, living out the Baptismal Covenant is a multifaceted journey that encompasses faith, repentance, proclamation, and service. It is a commitment to a life shaped by the teachings of Christ, marked by love, compassion, and a dedication to the well-being of others. This journey is not without its challenges, but it is through these challenges that faith is tested and strengthened. As believers navigate this spiritual odyssey, they find themselves drawn deeper into the transformative power of the Christian faith, living out the covenant in every facet of their lives.

Sanctification & Growth Unveil

Sanctification and growth are integral concepts in various religious, spiritual, and philosophical traditions. These terms often carry distinct meanings depending on the context in which they are used. Let's delve deeper into the understanding of sanctification and growth.

Sanctification:

Sanctification generally refers to the process of being made holy or set apart. This concept is deeply rooted in religious and theological contexts, particularly within Christianity. In Christian theology, sanctification is seen as a progressive transformation into the likeness of God or Christ. It involves the purification of the believer's heart and the development of virtues such as love, patience, and humility.

Christian Perspective:

Biblical Basis: The Bible plays a central role in shaping the understanding of sanctification. Passages like 1 Thessalonians 4:3, which states, "For this is the will of God, your sanctification," emphasize the divine desire for believers to be set apart for a holy purpose.

Process of Purification: Sanctification is often viewed as a lifelong process where individuals cooperate with the work of the Holy Spirit to overcome sin and grow in spiritual maturity. It involves a continual turning away from sinful behaviors and a pursuit of righteousness.

Means of Grace: Various means of grace, such as prayer, reading Scripture, participating in the sacraments, and engaging in acts of service, are considered essential in the journey of sanctification. These practices are believed to foster a deeper connection with the divine and contribute to personal transformation.

Comparative Religious Perspectives:

Islam: In Islam, the concept of sanctification aligns with the idea of purification (Tazkiyah). It involves cleansing the soul from impurities and cultivating virtues like sincerity and gratitude.

Judaism: Sanctification in Judaism is often associated with the idea of being set apart for a sacred purpose. Observance of religious rituals and adherence to moral laws contribute to this process.

Growth:

Growth, in a broader sense, refers to the process of development and maturation. It is not confined to religious or spiritual contexts but extends to various aspects of human life, including personal, intellectual, and emotional dimensions.

Personal Growth:

Self-Discovery: Personal growth often begins with self-discovery, gaining a deeper understanding of one's values, strengths, and areas for improvement. This self-awareness serves as a foundation for subsequent development.

Challenges and Learning: Growth is frequently catalyzed by facing challenges and learning from experiences. Overcoming obstacles, whether they are personal, professional, or relational, fosters resilience and contributes to overall development.

Intellectual Growth:

Continuous Learning: Intellectual growth involves a commitment to lifelong learning. Whether through formal education, reading, or engaging in intellectual discussions, individuals can expand their knowledge and understanding of the world.

Critical Thinking: The ability to think critically and analyze information is a crucial aspect of intellectual growth. It empowers individuals to evaluate situations, make informed decisions, and navigate complex issues.

Spiritual Growth:

Connection with the Divine: Spiritual growth, while related to sanctification in religious contexts, extends beyond specific religious beliefs. It encompasses the deepening of one's connection with the transcendent, however that may be conceptualized.

Mindfulness and Reflection: Practices like mindfulness and reflection contribute to spiritual growth by fostering a heightened awareness of the present moment and encouraging contemplation on life's deeper questions.

Interconnectedness:

Sanctification and growth are interconnected in profound ways. In religious frameworks, sanctification is often viewed as a form of spiritual growth, where individuals mature in their faith and character. However, growth is not exclusive to religious contexts; it is a universal concept that applies to various facets of human existence.

Overlapping Elements:

Virtue Development: Both sanctification and growth involve the development of virtues and positive qualities. Whether it's cultivating love, compassion, patience, or wisdom, individuals strive to embody these virtues in their journey of sanctification and growth.

Lifelong Journey: Neither sanctification nor growth is a one-time event. Both are considered lifelong processes that require commitment, effort, and a willingness to adapt and change over time.

Conclusion:

In conclusion, sanctification and growth are multifaceted concepts that hold significance across religious, spiritual, and secular domains. Whether viewed through the lens of religious transformation or personal development, both concepts share common elements such as the pursuit of virtue, resilience in the face of challenges, and a commitment to lifelong learning. Understanding and embracing sanctification and growth can lead to a more enriched and purposeful existence, contributing to the holistic well-being of individuals and communities.

Chapter 8: Contemporary Challenges and Questions

Contemporary challenges and questions surrounding baptism reflect the evolving landscape of religious practices and beliefs. As society undergoes cultural shifts, individuals grapple with the significance and implications of this sacrament in various religious traditions. Exploring these challenges requires a nuanced examination of theological, social, and ethical dimensions.

One key challenge revolves around the diversity of interpretations of baptism within Christianity. Different denominations and theological perspectives hold varying views on the mode of baptism (immersion, pouring, or sprinkling), the age at which it should be administered, and its salvific efficacy. This diversity raises questions about the unity of the Christian faith and the extent to which doctrinal differences should impact interdenominational relations.

The ecumenical movement, which seeks to foster unity among Christian denominations, also faces challenges related to baptism. Questions arise about whether differences in baptismal theology should be minimized for the sake of unity or if maintaining distinct practices is essential to denominational identity. This challenge reflects broader discussions within Christianity about the balance between unity and diversity in religious expression.

Another contemporary concern is the role of inclusivity and diversity in baptismal practices. As societies become more pluralistic, there is a growing awareness of the need for religious inclusivity. Questions emerge about how baptism, often seen as an initiation into a specific religious community, can be reconciled with the desire to respect and include individuals from diverse backgrounds. This challenge prompts theological reflections on the nature of belonging and community in the context of baptism.

Ethical considerations also play a significant role in contemporary discussions on baptism. Issues such as consent, especially concerning infant baptism, raise questions about the autonomy and agency of individuals within religious communities. Furthermore, the ecological crisis prompts reflection on the use of water in baptism and the ethical responsibility of religious communities in environmental stewardship.

The intersection of technology and religious practices introduces another set of challenges. With virtual communities becoming more prevalent, questions arise about the validity of online baptisms and whether physical presence is a necessary element of the sacrament. This challenge extends to the broader implications of digitization on religious rituals and the potential impact on the communal aspect of religious life.

Social justice concerns also influence contemporary debates on baptism. As religious institutions confront issues of inequality and injustice, questions emerge about the role of baptism in addressing societal problems. Some argue for a renewed emphasis on the ethical dimensions of baptism, viewing it as a call to social action and justice. This challenge prompts reflections on the role of religious rituals in shaping moral and ethical behavior.

The increasing secularization of society contributes to the challenges surrounding baptism. As religious affiliations decline in some regions, questions arise about the relevance and meaning of baptism in a secular context. This challenge prompts religious communities to articulate the enduring significance of baptism and its relevance to individuals who may not identify with traditional religious frameworks.

In conclusion, contemporary challenges and questions surrounding baptism reflect the dynamic nature of religious beliefs and practices in the modern era. The diversity of interpretations, the quest for inclusivity, ethical considerations, technological advancements, social justice concerns, and the impact of secularization all contribute to a complex landscape of reflection and dialogue within religious communities. Navigating these challenges requires a thoughtful engagement with theology, ethics, and the evolving dynamics of society.

Modern Obstacles to Baptism

1. Secularism:

In an increasingly secular world, traditional religious practices face skepticism and reduced significance. Many individuals today prioritize secular values over religious rituals, making baptism less appealing or relevant to a significant portion of the population.

2. Individualism:

Modern society often emphasizes individual autonomy and personal choice. This can lead people to question or reject practices like baptism, which may be viewed as imposing a communal or institutional identity rather than allowing individuals to determine their beliefs and affiliations independently.

3. Diversity of Beliefs:

The globalized world has facilitated the exchange of diverse cultural and religious ideas. This diversity can create challenges for traditional baptism practices, as individuals may be exposed to a wide range of beliefs and may find it difficult to commit to a specific religious tradition.

4. Scientific Rationalism:

Advancements in science and technology have contributed to a worldview rooted in empirical evidence and rational thinking. Some may find it challenging to reconcile traditional religious rituals, including baptism, with a scientific understanding of the world, leading to a decline in the practice.

5. Changing Family Structures:

Traditional family structures have evolved, and many individuals may come from non-traditional families or single-parent households. This shift can impact the likelihood of baptism, as the traditional understanding of baptism often involves a family or community context that may not align with modern family structures.

6. Social Stigma:

In certain societies or communities, there may be a social stigma associated with religious practices, including baptism. This stigma can deter individuals from openly expressing their religious beliefs or participating in religious ceremonies, hindering the acceptance and practice of baptism.

7. Lack of Religious Education:

In some cases, a lack of comprehensive religious education can contribute to a decreased understanding of the significance of baptism. Without a clear understanding of the ritual's meaning and importance, individuals may not see the relevance of undergoing the process.

8. Busy Lifestyles:

Modern life is often fast-paced, with individuals juggling multiple responsibilities such as work, education, and personal pursuits. This busyness may leave little time for religious involvement or reflection, making it challenging for individuals to prioritize and engage in religious rituals like baptism.

9. Skepticism Towards Institutions:

Growing skepticism towards religious institutions and their practices can act as a barrier to baptism. Individuals may be hesitant to engage in rituals associated with organized religion, viewing them as outdated or disconnected from their personal values.

10. Influence of Popular Culture:

The pervasive influence of popular culture, media, and entertainment can shape societal attitudes and norms. If popular culture tends to downplay or mock religious rituals, including baptism, individuals may be less inclined to embrace such practices.

In conclusion, while baptism remains a significant religious ceremony for many, various modern obstacles challenge its widespread acceptance and practice. Understanding and addressing these challenges requires a nuanced approach that considers the evolving nature of society and individuals' beliefs.

Ecumenical and Interfaith Issues

Ecumenical and interfaith issues encompass a broad spectrum of topics related to the dialogue, collaboration, and understanding among different religious traditions. The term "ecumenical" typically refers to efforts within Christianity to promote unity among various denominations, while "interfaith" extends beyond Christianity to include dialogue between different world religions. Both concepts share the common goal of fostering mutual respect, cooperation, and peace among diverse religious communities.

One key aspect of ecumenical and interfaith dialogue is the recognition of the rich diversity within and between religious traditions. This diversity encompasses theological beliefs, rituals, practices, and interpretations of sacred texts as long as it does not go against the teachings of Jesus Christ. Embracing this diversity is crucial for fostering meaningful dialogue that goes beyond mere tolerance to genuine understanding and appreciation of each other's faith perspectives.

Interfaith and ecumenical discussions often revolve around theological differences and similarities. Theological discussions delve into fundamental questions about the nature of God, the purpose of human existence, and the understanding of salvation or enlightenment. Scholars and religious leaders engage in deep theological conversations to identify common ground and bridge gaps that may exist between different faith traditions.

Historically, ecumenical efforts within Christianity have sought to overcome denominational divisions that emerged over theological, doctrinal, or cultural differences. The ecumenical movement, which gained momentum in the 20th century, has led to increased cooperation and understanding among Christian denominations. Efforts such as the World Council of Churches have played a significant role in promoting unity and addressing common concerns like social justice, peace, and human rights.

In contrast, interfaith dialogue involves interactions between different religious traditions, including but not limited to Christianity. This broader scope encompasses conversations between Islam, Judaism, Hinduism, Buddhism, Sikhism, and various other religious traditions. Interfaith dialogue aims to build bridges of understanding, tolerance, and cooperation, recognizing the shared values and ethical principles that underpin diverse faiths while helping one another understand the will of God for them.

One of the challenges in ecumenical and interfaith discussions is navigating the tension between preserving the distinctiveness of each tradition and finding common ground for cooperation. Striking this balance requires a delicate approach that acknowledges the uniqueness of each faith while fostering a spirit of inclusivity and collaboration.

Social and cultural contexts significantly influence ecumenical and interfaith dynamics. In pluralistic societies, where multiple religious traditions coexist, the need for interfaith understanding becomes even more pronounced. Such contexts provide opportunities for shared endeavors in addressing societal challenges, promoting peace, and contributing to the common good.

Promoting peace and addressing social issues are often areas where ecumenical and interfaith collaboration can make a tangible impact. Religious communities, when working together, can amplify their efforts to combat poverty, promote human rights, and contribute to environmental sustainability. By emphasizing shared values such as compassion, justice, and solidarity, ecumenical and interfaith initiatives can serve as powerful catalysts for positive change in the broader community.

Despite the positive aspects of ecumenical and interfaith dialogue, there are also challenges and barriers that must be acknowledged. Deep-seated historical conflicts, doctrinal differences, and cultural misunderstandings can pose significant obstacles to meaningful collaboration. Overcoming these challenges requires patience, empathy, and a commitment to building relationships over time.

Education plays a crucial role in fostering ecumenical and interfaith understanding. Schools, religious institutions, and community organizations can contribute to creating an environment where individuals learn about various faith traditions, their histories, and their contemporary expressions. This educational approach can dispel stereotypes, reduce prejudice, and promote a more inclusive and pluralistic society.

In conclusion, ecumenical and interfaith issues are complex and multifaceted, encompassing theological, social, and cultural dimensions. Meaningful dialogue and collaboration among different religious traditions can contribute to a more harmonious and interconnected world. While challenges exist, the potential benefits of fostering understanding, tolerance, and cooperation among diverse faith communities are significant and far-reaching.

Responding to Skeptics

Baptism is a significant sacrament in many Christian denominations, symbolizing spiritual rebirth and initiation into the faith. Skeptics may question its efficacy or necessity, often raising concerns about its historical origins, theological implications, or practical outcomes.

Historically, baptism finds its roots in various religious traditions and practices. In Christianity, it has been practiced since the time of John the Baptist and holds a central place in the New Testament. Some skeptics might question the consistency of baptism across denominations, pointing to differences in modes (immersion, pouring, or sprinkling) or the age at which individuals are baptized (infant or adult). Addressing these concerns involves delving into theological interpretations and historical developments within different Christian communities.

Theological perspectives on baptism vary widely among Christian traditions. Some view it as a symbolic act, representing the cleansing of sins and the believer's identification with Christ's death and resurrection. Others see it as a means of grace, conveying God's redemptive work in the life of the individual. Skeptics might challenge these theological viewpoints, questioning the spiritual significance attributed to a physical ritual. Clarifying the theological underpinnings and addressing biblical references that support baptism is crucial in responding to such skepticism.

Practical outcomes of baptism are also a subject of scrutiny. Skeptics may question whether the ritual genuinely transforms individuals or if it serves more as a cultural or social practice. Discussing personal testimonies, theological arguments, and historical examples can contribute to a comprehensive response. Additionally, exploring the impact of baptism on community identity and shared beliefs can shed light on its broader significance beyond individual experiences.

Engaging with skeptics requires a nuanced understanding of the diverse perspectives on baptism. A thoughtful response involves weaving together historical, theological, and practical elements, providing a robust defense of the sacrament's importance within the context of Christian faith.

Chapter 9: Practical Guidance

Practical guidance on baptism is an essential aspect of many religious traditions, symbolizing initiation, purification, and spiritual rebirth. Baptism holds significant meaning and rituals across various faiths, including Christianity, Judaism, and Islam. In this extensive exploration, we will delve into the practical aspects of baptism, examining its theological foundations, preparation, ceremony, and post-baptism considerations.

Theological Foundations:

Baptism's theological significance varies among religious traditions. In Christianity, particularly within Catholicism, Protestantism, and Orthodox Christianity, baptism is often considered a sacrament marking the initiation into the Christian faith. It is rooted in biblical narratives, such as the baptism of Jesus by John the Baptist in the Jordan River, symbolizing purification and spiritual rebirth.

Preparation for Baptism:

Choosing Godparents or Sponsors:

In many Christian traditions, individuals being baptized have godparents or sponsors who play a vital role in their spiritual journey. Godparents are chosen to provide support, guidance, and spiritual mentorship. The selection of godparents is a thoughtful process, often involving individuals who are committed to the religious upbringing of the baptized person.

Ceremonial Aspects:

The baptismal ceremony varies among Christian denominations but generally includes essential elements such as the blessing of water, the renunciation of sin, and the profession of faith. The symbolism of water is crucial, representing purification and the washing away of sins. The mode of baptism can differ, with some traditions practicing immersion, while others use pouring or sprinkling.

Attire and Symbols:

Attire for baptism varies across cultures and denominations. White robes are commonly used, symbolizing purity and the new life in Christ. Other symbols, such as candles and anointing oils, may also play a role in the ceremony, signifying the enlightenment and empowerment of the Holy Spirit.

Post-Baptism Considerations:

After the baptism ceremony, there are ongoing considerations for the individual and their family. Continuing religious education, participation in the faith community, and the practice of spiritual disciplines are emphasized. Regular attendance at worship services and engagement with the sacraments further solidify the individual's connection to their faith.

Diversity in Baptismal Practices:

While there are commonalities, baptismal practices vary widely among different Christian denominations and other religious traditions. Some denominations practice believer's baptism, where individuals are baptized upon a personal confession of faith. Others, like infant baptism, emphasize God's grace and covenant relationship with the entire community.

Challenges and Controversies:

Despite the significance of baptism, there are occasional controversies and debates within religious communities. Differences in theological understanding, the age of baptismal candidates, and the mode of baptism can lead to discussions and disagreements. However, many faith traditions encourage respectful dialogue to foster understanding and unity.

Interfaith Perspectives:

Baptism is not exclusive to Christianity; it has parallels in other religions. In Judaism, the mikvah serves as a ritual bath for purification, while Islam practices a form of ablution called "wudu" before prayer. Exploring these interfaith connections can deepen one's understanding of the shared human inclination toward spiritual purification and renewal.

In conclusion, practical guidance on baptism encompasses a broad spectrum of theological, ceremonial, and post-baptismal considerations. Understanding the significance of baptism within a specific religious tradition, preparing for the ceremony, and embracing the ongoing spiritual journey are integral aspects of this transformative sacrament. Whether through the immersion in water, the pouring of water, or other symbolic acts, baptism remains a profound and universally recognized expression of faith and commitment.

Choosing Sponsors and Witnesses

Selecting sponsors and witnesses for a baptism is a significant aspect of the ceremony, as they play vital roles in supporting and guiding the individual being baptized. The process involves careful consideration and reflection to ensure that those chosen are spiritually mature and committed to their roles. Here, we'll delve into the various factors to consider when choosing sponsors and witnesses for baptism.

Firstly, sponsors, also known as godparents, are individuals who take on the responsibility of guiding the baptized person in their faith journey. Traditionally, they are chosen from the close circle of family and friends, often people who hold a strong connection to the religious community. When selecting sponsors, it's crucial to assess their commitment to the faith and their ability to serve as positive role models for the one being baptized.

The spiritual maturity of sponsors is paramount. Ideally, sponsors should be individuals who actively practice their faith, regularly attend religious services, and demonstrate a deep understanding of the principles and teachings of the religion. This ensures that they can provide meaningful guidance to the individual being baptized and help nurture their spiritual growth.

Additionally, sponsors should possess a genuine love and concern for the well-being of the baptized person. Their role extends beyond the baptism ceremony, involving ongoing support and encouragement in the individual's faith journey. Choosing sponsors who genuinely care about the spiritual development of the baptized person strengthens the foundation of the mentorship relationship.

Another crucial consideration is the lifestyle of potential sponsors. It's essential to select individuals whose lives align with the moral and ethical values of the religious community. Sponsors should be individuals who strive to live virtuously and serve as examples of how to integrate faith into daily life. This consistency between beliefs and actions enhances the credibility of the sponsors and reinforces the positive influence they can have on the baptized individual.

In some religious traditions, there may be specific requirements for sponsors, such as being baptized themselves or belonging to the same denomination. It's essential to adhere to these guidelines to ensure that the sponsors are recognized as suitable role models within the religious community.

Witnesses, while not always a formal part of the baptism ceremony, can still hold significance in the process. They are individuals who bear witness to the baptism and often play a supportive role in the faith community. Similar to sponsors, witnesses should be chosen based on their commitment to the faith and their ability to provide positive encouragement.

When selecting witnesses, consider individuals who have a strong connection to the religious community and a genuine interest in the well-being of the person being baptized. Their presence adds to the communal aspect of the ceremony, creating a supportive environment for the individual taking this significant step in their faith journey.

In conclusion, choosing sponsors and witnesses for baptism is a thoughtful and meaningful process. It involves considering factors such as spiritual maturity, commitment to the faith, lifestyle alignment, and the ability to serve as positive role models. By carefully selecting individuals who embody these qualities, the baptism ceremony becomes not only a symbolic initiation into the faith but also the beginning of a supportive and nurturing spiritual community for the baptized person.

Baptismal Services and Rituals

Baptismal Rituals Across Cultures:

Baptismal services and rituals hold significant cultural, religious, and personal importance across various traditions and faiths. The act of baptism symbolizes purification, initiation, and the spiritual rebirth of an individual. This sacred ceremony is conducted in diverse ways, each carrying its unique customs and meanings.

In Christianity, baptism is a sacrament that signifies the initiation into the Christian faith. The ritual involves the use of water to cleanse the individual from sin, following the example of Jesus Christ's baptism in the Jordan River. Denominations within Christianity may differ in their practices, but common elements often include the use of holy water, prayers, and the recitation of specific liturgical passages.

Catholicism, for instance, incorporates baptism into the broader framework of initiation sacraments, which also include confirmation and the Eucharist. The Catholic baptismal rite typically involves the pouring or immersion of water on the forehead of the person being baptized, even though there is no biblical proof in the Newt Testament for water to be on the forehead, accompanied by the Trinitarian formula invoking the Father, Son, and Holy Spirit.

In Eastern Orthodox Christianity, baptism is considered one of the Mysteries, or sacraments, and is often administered through triple immersion in water. The immersion represents a burial and resurrection with Christ, emphasizing the transformative nature of the sacrament.

Protestant denominations vary in their baptismal practices. Some, like Baptists, emphasize believer's baptism, where individuals make a conscious decision to be baptized after professing their faith. Other Protestant traditions, such as Lutherans or Anglicans, practice infant baptism, where infants are baptized as a symbol of God's grace and covenant with the community.

Beyond Christianity, baptismal rituals are found in other religions. In Islam, a form of ritual purification known as "Ghusl" bears similarities to the concept of spiritual cleansing found in baptism. However, Islam does not have a direct equivalent to the Christian sacrament.

In Hinduism, various purification rituals are performed, and water holds a symbolic significance in many ceremonies. While there isn't a direct equivalent to Christian baptism, the concept of ritual purification and initiation into spiritual practices is prevalent.

Judaism, too, has immersion rituals, such as the "mikveh," which is a ritual bath used for various purposes, including purification. Although not equivalent to Christian baptism, the mikveh shares similarities in the use of water for spiritual cleansing.

In African and indigenous religions, water is often a central element in purification rituals and rites of passage. These rituals vary widely across different cultures, reflecting the diversity of beliefs and practices within these traditions.

In contemporary secular contexts, baptismal-like ceremonies are also observed in non-religious settings. These may take the form of naming ceremonies, commitment ceremonies, or other rites symbolizing a new beginning or transition.

The symbolism of baptism extends beyond religious contexts. Water, as a universal symbol of life and cleansing, connects diverse cultures and belief systems. The act of immersion or pouring water during baptism represents a profound transformation, a washing away of the old and a welcoming of the new.

In conclusion, baptismal services and rituals are rich in symbolism and cultural significance, transcending religious boundaries. Whether in the context of Christianity, Islam, Hinduism, Judaism, or indigenous traditions, the act of baptism serves as a powerful symbol of spiritual rebirth, purification, and initiation into a community or faith. The diverse ways in which this ritual is practiced reflect the depth of human spirituality and the universal importance of symbolic acts in marking significant transitions in life.

But only immersion was practiced:

In the New Testament, the practice of immersion in water for baptism is a significant and recurring theme. The act of baptism, often symbolizing spiritual purification, repentance, and initiation into the Christian faith, is primarily associated with immersion in water. While various forms of baptism are mentioned in the Bible, including John the Baptist's baptisms and the baptism of the Holy Spirit, immersion remains a prominent mode throughout the New Testament.

One of the earliest accounts of baptism in the New Testament is found in the Gospels, where John the Baptist plays a central role. In the Gospel of Matthew, for instance, John baptizes people in the Jordan River, and Jesus himself undergoes baptism in this manner. The text describes how Jesus came up out of the water, reinforcing the idea of immersion as a central element in the baptismal ritual.

The Gospel of Mark similarly narrates John the Baptist's baptisms in the Jordan River, emphasizing the immersion of individuals in the water. The Gospel of Luke, too, provides an account of John's baptisms, portraying the act as a cleansing ritual involving immersion.

The Apostle Paul, in his letters to various early Christian communities, further reinforces the significance of immersion in water for baptism. In his letter to the Romans, Paul writes about being buried with Christ through baptism into death, emphasizing the immersion imagery as a symbolic burial and resurrection. The language used by Paul suggests a deep connection between the act of immersion and the spiritual transformation it represents.

The First Epistle to the Corinthians also contains references to baptism, with Paul using language that implies immersion. He speaks of being baptized into one body, again underscoring the immersive nature of the ritual and its role in unifying believers.

The Book of Acts, a historical account of the early Christian church, provides additional instances of immersion in water for baptism. In Acts 8, Philip baptizes the Ethiopian eunuch by going down into the water with him, and in Acts 10, Peter baptizes Cornelius and his household. Both accounts suggest the practice of immersion, aligning with the broader theme in the New Testament.

While immersion is the predominant mode of baptism depicted in the New Testament, it is essential to acknowledge that the Bible also mentions other forms of baptism. For instance, the Gospel of John describes a type of baptism involving the Holy Spirit, separate from water baptism. However, it's important to note that these variations do not diminish the emphasis on immersion in the overall narrative of baptism within the New Testament.

The theological significance of immersion in water for baptism is rooted in its symbolism. The act of being submerged and then emerging from the water is seen as a powerful representation of dying to one's old self and rising to a new life in Christ. This symbolism aligns with the Christian belief in the death and resurrection of Jesus, making immersion a fitting expression of spiritual rebirth and renewal.

The New Testament's consistent portrayal of immersion in water for baptism underscores its importance as a central rite in early Christian communities. The act's symbolic depth, coupled with its historical continuity in the biblical narrative, has contributed to the enduring practice of immersion in various Christian denominations today. As believers engage in this sacrament, they not only participate in a ritual established by Jesus and practiced by early Christians but also affirm their commitment to a life of faith and discipleship.

Luke 7:30 is a verse from the New Testament of the Bible, and it reads, "But the Pharisees and the lawyers rejected the purpose of God for themselves, not having been baptized by him." This verse is part of a larger narrative where Jesus reflects on the reactions of the people to John the Baptist and himself.

To elaborate further, this verse highlights the resistance and rejection faced by Jesus from certain religious authorities of his time, specifically the Pharisees and lawyers. The phrase "rejected the purpose of God for themselves" suggests a deliberate choice to oppose or disregard the divine message that Jesus brought.

In a broader context, this rejection can be seen as a recurring theme in the Bible and religious narratives, where prophets or messengers encounter resistance from those entrenched in established religious practices or authority structures. This resistance often stems from a reluctance to embrace new teachings or challenges to existing beliefs.

Drawing parallels to today's world, this rejection of new ideas or perspectives is not limited to historical religious contexts. In various aspects of modern society, we observe resistance to change, whether it be in scientific theories, social norms, or political ideologies. The human tendency to cling to familiar beliefs and resist challenges to established norms is a common thread that connects historical narratives with contemporary experiences.

For example, consider the rejection of certain scientific theories despite overwhelming evidence, the resistance to social progress, or the dismissal of alternative perspectives in political discourse. These instances mirror the Pharisees and lawyers' rejection of Jesus' message, illustrating how the human inclination to resist change persists across time and contexts.

In essence, Luke 7:30 serves as a reminder of the challenges faced by those who bring forth new ideas or perspectives, emphasizing the enduring nature of resistance to change in human societies. This biblical verse prompts reflection on how individuals and communities can approach innovation, differing viewpoints, and transformative ideas in the present day.

Baptism as the counsel of God

Baptism, as understood through the lens of Luke 7:30, is a significant concept within Christian theology. In Luke 7:30, the scripture states, "But the Pharisees and the lawyers rejected the purpose of God for themselves, not having been baptized by him." This verse encapsulates the theme of baptism as a divine counsel, illustrating a rejection of God's purpose by those who did not undergo baptism.

To delve deeper into the meaning of baptism as the counsel of God, we must explore the broader theological context and biblical foundations. Baptism is a sacrament widely practiced in Christianity, signifying purification, regeneration, and initiation into the faith community. The understanding of baptism varies among Christian denominations, but Luke 7:30 sheds light on the significance of this ritual as a divine directive.

In the broader context of the Bible, baptism is often associated with repentance, forgiveness of sins, and the reception of the Holy Spirit. John the Baptist, a central figure in the New Testament, is recognized for baptizing people in the Jordan River, preparing them for the coming of the Messiah. Jesus himself underwent baptism, setting an example for his followers and emphasizing the importance of this act.

The theological implications of baptism as the counsel of God are rooted in the belief that through this ritual, individuals align themselves with God's purpose and enter into a covenant relationship with Him. Baptism symbolizes a spiritual rebirth, a transition from a state of separation from God to one of reconciliation and grace. The rejection of baptism, as highlighted in Luke 7:30, signifies a resistance to God's intended plan for salvation and spiritual transformation.

Moreover, baptism is often viewed as a public declaration of faith. It serves as a visible and symbolic representation of an individual's commitment to follow Christ. The immersion in water symbolizes the burial of the old self and the emergence of a new life in Christ. This symbolism aligns with the biblical narrative of death and resurrection, mirroring the transformative power of God's counsel through baptism.

BAPTISM A BIBLICAL EXPLORATION

The Gospel of Luke, in particular, emphasizes themes of repentance, mercy, and inclusion. The rejection of God's purpose by the Pharisees and lawyers, who did not undergo baptism, underscores the importance of humility and openness to God's guidance. Baptism becomes a pivotal moment of surrender to divine counsel, a response to the call of God to enter into a deeper relationship with Him.

In the early Christian community, baptism played a central role in the process of conversion. The Book of Acts records numerous instances where individuals and households were baptized upon hearing the message of salvation. The apostles, following the Great Commission given by Jesus, baptized new believers, underscoring the universal nature of this sacrament as a means of incorporating individuals into the body of Christ.

As the Christian Church developed its theological understanding over the centuries, various theological perspectives on baptism emerged. Some denominations emphasize infant baptism as a means of initiating children into the faith, while others advocate for believer's baptism, asserting that individuals should be baptized only after making a personal profession of faith. Despite these differences, the foundational concept of baptism as a response to God's counsel remains a unifying thread within Christianity.

In conclusion, Luke 7:30 provides a succinct yet profound insight into the significance of baptism as the counsel of God. This verse invites believers to reflect on their own response to God's purpose and the role of baptism in aligning with divine guidance. The broader biblical narrative supports the understanding of baptism as a transformative and sacramental act that signifies a commitment to God's redemptive plan. Whether through the repentance preached by John the Baptist or the example set by Jesus, baptism stands as a tangible expression of faith and a response to the divine counsel presented in scripture.

Conclusion

Summarizing Key Points: Baptism is a Christian sacrament involving water, symbolizing purification and initiation into the faith. Key points include its significance in various Christian denominations, the ritual's connection to Jesus' baptism, and its role in spiritual rebirth and forgiveness of sins.

Baptism is a profound symbol of spiritual rebirth and commitment. As you contemplate this sacred act, envision the cleansing waters as a source of renewal, washing away old burdens and ushering in a new chapter of faith. Embrace the significance of baptism as a public declaration of your dedication to a higher purpose. Just as water purifies, let this ritual purify your heart, fostering a deeper connection with your spiritual journey.

Remember, baptism is not merely a ritual but a transformative experience, marking the beginning of a life guided by principles of love, compassion, and humility. Trust in the power of this sacrament to strengthen your resolve in times of challenge, serving as a constant reminder of your identity within a supportive spiritual community. Approach this moment with joy and anticipation, for through baptism, you forge a lasting bond with your faith, and may your path be illuminated with the divine light that baptism represents.

Call to Embrace Baptism

And finally, Embrace the transformative waters of baptism, a sacred initiation into a community bound by faith. In the gentle embrace of baptismal waters, experience the profound symbolism of rebirth, cleansing the soul from sin, and emerging anew in the embrace of divine grace. Let the act of baptism be a declaration of your commitment to a spiritual journey, a surrender to a higher purpose that transcends earthly concerns. It is an invitation to join a community of believers, a family united by shared values and a common faith. Embracing baptism signifies a profound connection to a timeless tradition, an affirmation of spiritual identity, and a conscious step toward a life guided by the principles of love, compassion, and faith.

As you immerse yourself in the sacred ritual of baptism, may it be a poignant reminder of the eternal covenant between the individual and the divine—a call to walk the path of righteousness with unwavering devotion.

Milton Keynes UK
Ingram Content Group UK Ltd.
UKHW010932231123
433129UK00001B/82

9 798215 085844